TABLE OF CONTENTS

INTRODUCTION

1.	It is with great pleasure that the Government of the United States of America presents its Periodic Report to the United Nations Committee Against Torture concerning the implementation of its obligations under the Convention Against Torture and Other Cruel, Inhuman or Degrading Treatment or Punishment (hereinafter referred to as "Convention" or "CAT"), pursuant to Article 19 of the Convention. This document constitutes the third, fourth, and fifth periodic reports of the United States.

2.	The absolute prohibition of torture is of fundamental importance to the United States. As President Obama stated in his address to the nation on national security, delivered at the National Archives on May 21, 2009: "I can stand here today, as President of the United States, and say without exception or equivocation that we do not torture, and that we will vigorously protect our people while forging a strong and durable framework that allows us to fight terrorism while abiding by the rule of law." Most recently, in his May 23, 2013 speech at the National Defense University, the President reiterated that the United States has "unequivocally banned torture."

3.	Marking the anniversary of the CAT's adoption on June 24, 2011, President Obama noted that, more than two decades ago, President Reagan signed and a bipartisan coalition provided Senate advice and consent to ratification of the Convention, "which affirms the essential principle that under no circumstances is torture ever justified." President Obama continued:

> . . . Torture and abusive treatment violate our most deeply held values, and they do not enhance our national security – they undermine it by serving as a recruiting tool for terrorists and further endangering the lives of American personnel. Furthermore, torture and other forms of cruel, inhuman or degrading treatment are ineffective at developing useful, accurate information. As President, I have therefore made it clear that the United States will prohibit torture without exception or equivocation, and I reaffirmed our commitment to the Convention's tenets and our domestic laws.

As a nation that played a leading role in the effort to bring this treaty into force, the United States will remain a leader in the effort to end torture around the world and to address the needs of torture victims. We continue to support the United Nations Voluntary Fund for Victims of Torture, and to provide funding for domestic and international programs that provide assistance and counseling for torture victims. We also remain dedicated to supporting the efforts of other nations, as well as international and nongovernmental organizations, to eradicate torture through human rights training for security forces, improving prison and detention conditions, and encouraging the development and enforcement of strong laws that outlaw this abhorrent practice.

The full text of the President's statement is available at www.whitehouse.gov/the-press-office/2011/06/24/statement-president-international-day-support-victims-torture.

4.   Treaty reporting is a way in which the Government of the United States can inform its citizens and the international community of its efforts to ensure the implementation of those obligations it has assumed, while at the same time holding itself up to the public scrutiny of the international community and civil society. In preparing this report, the United States has taken the opportunity to engage in a process of stock-taking and self-examination. Representatives of U.S. government agencies involved in implementation of the Convention met with representatives of non-governmental organizations as part of outreach efforts to civil society in this process. The United States has instituted this process as part of its efforts to improve its communication and consultation on human rights obligations and policies. Thus, this report is not an end in itself, but an important tool in the development of practical and effective human rights strategies by the U.S. government.

5.   This report was prepared by the U.S. Department of State (DOS) with extensive assistance from the U.S. Department of Justice (DOJ), the U.S. Department of Defense (DoD), the U.S. Department of Homeland Security (DHS), the U.S. Department of Education (ED) and other relevant components of the U.S. government. It responds to the 55 questions prepared by the Committee and transmitted to the United States on January 10, 2010 (CAT/C/USA/Q/5) pursuant to the new optional reporting procedure adopted by the Committee in May 2007 at its

38th Session (A/62/44). The information included in the responses supplements information included in the U.S. Initial Report (CAT/C/28/Add.5, February 9, 2000, hereinafter referred to as "Initial Report") and its Second Periodic Report (CAT/C/48/Add.3, June 29, 2005, hereinafter referred to as "2005 CAT Report"), and information provided by the United States in connection with Committee meetings considering the reports, including its 2006 Response to List of Issues (April 28, 2006, hereinafter referred to as "Response to List of Issues") and 2007 Follow-up (July 25, 2007). It also takes into account the Concluding Observations of the Committee Against Torture (CAT/C/USA/CO/2, July 25, 2006), as referenced in the questions provided by the Committee. Throughout the report, the United States has considered carefully views expressed by the Committee in its prior written communications and in its public sessions with the United States. A list of acronyms used in the report, and the full name of each, is attached as Annex B.

6.   In the spirit of cooperation, the United States has provided detailed and thorough answers to the questions posed by the Committee, whether or not the questions or information provided in response to them bear directly on obligations arising under the Convention. It should be noted that the report does not address the geographic scope of the Convention as a legal matter, although it does respond to related questions from the Committee in factual terms.

7.   The United States also directs the Committee's attention to the Fourth Periodic Report of the United States of America to the United Nations Committee on Human Rights Concerning the International Covenant on Civil and Political Rights filed in December 2011 (hereinafter referred to as "2011 ICCPR Report," available at www.state.gov/j/drl/rls/179781.htm) and the U.S. Periodic Report Concerning the International Convention on the Elimination of All Forms of Racial Discrimination filed in June 2013 (hereinafter referred to as "2013 CERD Report," available at www.state.gov/j/drl/rls/cerd_report/210605.htm). Although the United States has endeavored to fully answer each of the Committee's 55 questions in the text of this report, in a number of places the report also incorporates by reference sections of the 2011 ICCPR Report, the 2013 CERD Report, and the Common Core Document of the United States filed in December 2011 (hereinafter referred to as "CCD") in the interest of full and robust reporting.

PERIODIC REPORT OF THE
UNITED STATES OF AMERICA
August 5, 2013

Specific information on the implementation of articles 1 to 16 of the Convention, <u>including with regard to the previous recommendations of the Committee</u>

<u>Articles 1 and 4</u>

1. Please provide information on steps taken to enact a federal crime of torture consistent with article 1 of the Convention, which includes appropriate penalties, as recommended by the Committee in its previous concluding observations (para. 13).

8. All acts of torture are offenses under criminal law in the United States. The precise manner in which a State Party accomplishes this obligation is left for each State Party to decide for itself, as a matter of domestic law. The Convention does not require States Parties to enact a crime labeled "torture" per se, nor does it require a State with a federal system to satisfy its obligations fully through criminal laws at the federal level.

9. As described more fully in response to Questions 3, 7, 22, and 23, and in the Initial Report ¶¶ 45-50, 100-119 and 2005 CAT Report ¶¶ 11-19, in the United States acts of torture may be prosecuted in a variety of ways at both the federal and state level, for instance, as aggravated assault or battery or mayhem; homicide, murder or manslaughter; kidnapping; false imprisonment or abduction; rape, sodomy, or molestation; or as part of an attempt, a conspiracy, or a criminal violation of an individual's civil rights. In addition, some states have criminal torture statutes, not limited in their application to State actors. Furthermore, most, if not all, acts that would qualify as torture by State actors could be prosecuted under 18 U.S.C. 242 as deprivations of U.S. constitutional rights.

10. Before ratifying the Convention, the United States enacted a criminal torture statute (18 U.S.C. 2340A et seq.) to enable it to implement fully the obligations under Articles 5 and 7 (e.g., to ensure that all cases of torture committed by a United States national are criminalized).

11.   This legal landscape means that every act of torture within the meaning of the Convention is criminalized under federal and/or state law. Because existing law fully implements its obligations in this regard, the United States is not actively considering adopting new federal legislation to duplicate existing applicable laws.

2. Please clarify the State party's position with regard to its understanding of acts of psychological torture, prohibited by the Convention. Does the State party recognize a wider category of acts which cause severe mental suffering, irrespective of their prolongation or its duration, as acts of psychological torture prohibited by the Convention?

12.   As discussed in ¶ 95 of the Initial Report, the United States agrees that the intentional infliction of mental pain or suffering was appropriately included in the definition of torture to reflect the increasing and deplorable use by certain States of various psychological forms of torture and ill-treatment, such as mock executions, sensory deprivations, use of drugs, and confinement to mental hospitals. Psychological torture is redressable under the U.S. criminal laws discussed above, as well as under the Torture Victim Protection Act, 28 U.S.C. 1350 note. When the United States was considering becoming a State Party, there was some concern within the U.S. criminal justice community that the Convention's definition could not satisfy the constitutional requirement of precision in defining criminal offenses with respect to mental pain and suffering. To provide the requisite clarity for purposes of domestic law, the United States therefore conditioned its ratification upon an understanding that includes the statement that "mental pain or suffering refers to prolonged mental harm." This understanding recited elements implicit in the text to provide the specificity needed to meet the requirements of a criminal statute.

3. Please provide updated information on any changes in the State party's position that the Convention is not applicable at all times, whether in peace, war or armed conflict, in any territory under its jurisdiction and is not without prejudice to the provisions of any other international instrument, pursuant to article 1, paragraph 2, and 16, paragraph 2, of the Convention.

13.   Under U.S. law, officials of all government agencies are prohibited from engaging in torture, at all times, and in all places, not only in territory under U.S. jurisdiction. Under the Detainee Treatment Act of 2005 (DTA), Pub. L. No. 109-163, 42 U.S.C. 2000dd ("No individual in the custody or under the physical control of the U.S. Government, regardless of nationality or physical location, shall be subject to cruel, inhuman, or degrading treatment or punishment"),

every U.S. official, wherever he or she may be, is also prohibited from engaging in acts that constitute cruel, inhuman or degrading treatment or punishment. This prohibition is enforced at all levels of U.S. government.

14.   With respect to the application of the Convention and the international law of armed conflict (also referred to as international humanitarian law), Article 2(2) of the Convention specifically provides that neither "a state of war [n]or a threat of war … may be invoked as a justification for torture." Thus, in the view of the United States, a time of war does not suspend the operation of the Convention as to matters within its scope of application. Torture is clearly and categorically prohibited under an extensive body of both human rights law and the law of armed conflict. The obligation to prevent cruel, inhuman, or degrading treatment or punishment is also contained in Article 16 of the Convention and in similar provisions in the law of armed conflict. Executive Orders and other statements by President Obama addressing compliance with the CAT and other obligations to treat detainees humanely are discussed in response to Question 5 and elsewhere as relevant in this report.

Article 2

4. In light of the Committee's previous concluding observations (para. 16) and the replies provided in the State party's comments under the follow-up procedure (CAT/C/USA/CO/2/Add.1, para. 3), please provide:

(a) Information on steps taken by the State party to ensure that it registers all persons it detains in any territory under its jurisdiction, including in all areas under its de facto effective control. Please elaborate on whether steps have been taken to adopt legislative measures to make registration obligatory for all authorities, including military authorities. Please clarify in which cases the authorities do not maintain appropriate records on persons detained.
(b) Details of cases in which the registration of persons detained does not contain all the elements mentioned in paragraph 16 of the previous concluding observations as to guarantee an effective safeguard against acts of torture.

Response to issues raised in Question 4(a).
15.   Noting paragraph 6 of this Report, although there is no unified national policy governing the registry of all persons detained by the United States, relevant individual federal, state, and local authorities, including military authorities, maintain appropriate records on persons detained by them. Although the United States notes that the Convention has no provision requiring the

registration of detainees, such records would generally include the information mentioned in the Committee's recommendation.

16.   DoD keeps detailed information regarding every individual it detains, to serve as both an aid in ensuring appropriate care and custody and as an appropriate oversight mechanism of the conditions of detention. It also assigns internment serial numbers to all detainees interned by the United States in connection with armed conflict as soon as practicable and in all cases within 14 days of capture, and grants the International Committee of the Red Cross (ICRC) access to such detainees, consistent with DoD regulations and policies. Pursuant to DoD Directive 2310.01E (The DoD Detainee Program), the ICRC is made aware of and has access to all U.S. law of war detention facilities and all persons detained by the United States in situations of armed conflict. This is consistent with President Obama's Executive Order (E.O.) 13491 on Ensuring Lawful Interrogations, issued on January 22, 2009, requiring that all agencies of the U.S. government provide the ICRC with such notification of and access to any individual detained in any armed conflict in the custody or under the effective control of an officer, employee, or other agent of the U.S. government or detained within a facility owned, operated, or controlled by a department or agency of the U.S. government, consistent with DoD regulations and policies.

17.   Within the United States, the U.S. and state constitutions and other laws provide comprehensive safeguards to ensure that persons under detention are protected and provided due process. Under such laws, all persons detained are booked when they are taken into custody. Generally, booking information includes the name, physical description, charges, bond information, and emergency contact information for the detainee. Such bookings are public information and are often published in local newspapers. Pre-trial detention is governed by constitutional and statutory standards, and approved and supervised by independent judicial officers who are available to address allegations of mistreatment.

18.   Registration is further enhanced by the requirement for public court appearance for those detained for violation of federal, state or local criminal law. Persons arrested for federal offenses are generally brought before a judicial officer the day of arrest, or the following day if no judicial officer is available on the day that the individual is arrested. Furthermore, a confession obtained by federal authorities may be deemed inadmissible by a court if more than six hours elapse

between an arrest and a suspect's first court appearance if the only reason for delay was for interrogation. Corley v. United States, 556 U.S. 303 (2009). Taken together, these requirements are essential safeguards that a prisoner's status will be a matter of public record.

19.   Additionally, the DOJ Bureau of Prisons (BOP) provides information to the public concerning the whereabouts of those in detention through an online locator, available at www.bop.gov/iloc2/LocateInmate.jsp. A link to this resource is provided on the DOJ home page at www.justice.gov.

20.   DHS registers all individuals detained in immigration matters. The registration process is initiated when immigration officers have identified, located and apprehended aliens who have violated provisions of the Immigration and Nationality Act. Within DHS, U.S. Immigration and Customs Enforcement (ICE) operates a public web-based Online Detainee Locator System, available at https://locator.ice.gov/odls/homePage.do, that enables attorneys, family, and friends to find a detainee in ICE custody and to access information about the facility, including address and visiting hours.

21.   Most states also have their own locator systems for inmates held in state or local custody. A list of links to locators by state is available at http://answers.usa.gov/system/selfservice.controller?CONFIGURATION=1000&PARTITION_I D=1&CMD=VIEW_ARTICLE&USERTYPE=1&LANGUAGE. Links to assist in locating persons in local custody are available at www.usa.gov/Agencies/Local.shtml.

Response to issues raised in Question 4(b).
22.   The United States believes that the information it maintains on all detained persons is sufficient to provide an effective safeguard against violations of the Convention.

5. Please provide information on:

(a) Whether the State party has adopted a policy that ensures that no one is detained in any secret detention facility under its de facto effective control and that publicly condemns secret detention, pursuant the Committee's previous concluding observations (para. 17). Please disclose detailed information on the existence of any such facilities, in the past and present, and the authority under which they have been established. In this respect, please respond to allegations made by the Special Rapporteur on torture and other cruel, inhuman or degrading treatment or punishment and the

Council of Europe that the State party has used the British Indian Ocean Territory, Diego Garcia, for the secret detention of high-value "terror" suspects. [fn: M. Nowak, Associated Press, March 2008, and Council of Europe, "Secret detentions and illegal transfers of detainees involving Council of Europe member states: second report", 11 June 2007, para.70.]

       (b) The legal safeguards provided to the detainees and the manner in which they are treated.

       (c) Steps taken to address the reports of detainees held incommunicado and without the protection of domestic or international law (CCPR/C/USA/CO/3/Rev.1, para. 12). In this respect, please provide information on steps taken to ensure that all detained suspects, including in Diego Garcia and at Bagram Airbase in Afghanistan, are afforded, in practice, fundamental safeguards, including the right to a lawyer and an independent medical examination, as well as the right to inform a relative and have access to a court and the right to challenge the grounds for their detention.

Response to issues raised in Question 5(a).

23.   In September 2006 former President Bush acknowledged that in addition to individuals then held at the U.S. Naval Station Guantanamo Bay (Guantanamo), "a small number of suspected terrorist leaders and operatives captured during the war [were] held and questioned outside the United States, in a separate program operated by the Central Intelligence Agency." He then announced that 14 individuals were being transferred from Central Intelligence Agency (CIA) custody to DoD custody at Guantanamo. The CIA's overseas detention and interrogation program was described in detail in a 2004 CIA Inspector General Special Review, which has been publicly released in redacted form, and was further discussed in DOJ Office of Legal Counsel memoranda from 2002 and 2005 that were publicly released in 2009.

24.   On his second full day in office, January 22, 2009, President Obama issued three executive orders concerning lawful interrogations, the military detention facility at Guantanamo, and detention policy options. E.O. 13491, Ensuring Lawful Interrogations, instructed the CIA to close as expeditiously as possible any detention facilities it operated. As noted in the answer to Question 4, it requires that all agencies of the U.S. government provide the ICRC with timely access to any individual detained by the United States in any armed conflict, consistent with DoD regulations and policies.

25.   Consistent with E.O. 13491, the CIA does not operate any detention facilities. The United States does not have and has never had a detention facility on Diego Garcia.

26.   The United States does not operate any secret detention facilities. In some contexts, the United States operates battlefield transit and screening facilities, the locations of which are often classified for reasons of military necessity. All such facilities are operated consistent with applicable U.S. law and policy and international law, including Common Article 3 of the Geneva Conventions, the Detainee Treatment Act of 2005, and DoD Directive 2310.01E. The ICRC and relevant host governments are informed about these facilities, and the ICRC has access to all individuals interned by the United States in the context of armed conflict, consistent with DoD policy.

Response to issues raised in Question 5(b).

27.   Pursuant to E.O. 13491, all U.S. detention facilities in the context of armed conflict are operated consistent with obligations under U.S. domestic and international law and policy. E.O. 13491 directs that individuals detained in any armed conflict shall in all circumstances be treated humanely, consistent with U.S. domestic law, treaty obligations and U.S. policy, and shall not be subjected to violence to life and person (including murder of all kinds, mutilation, cruel treatment, and torture), nor to outrages upon personal dignity (including humiliating and degrading treatment), whenever such individuals are in the custody or under the effective control of an officer, employee, or other agent of the U.S. government or detained within a facility owned, operated, or controlled by a department or agency of the United States; and that such individuals shall not be subjected to any interrogation technique or approach, or any treatment related to interrogation, that is not authorized by and listed in the Army Field Manual on Human Intelligence Collector Operations, FM 2-22.3 (Army Field Manual), without prejudice to authorized non-coercive techniques of federal law enforcement agencies.

28.   In March 2011 the United States confirmed its support for Additional Protocol II and for Article 75 of Additional Protocol I to the 1949 Geneva Conventions. A March 7, 2011 White House press release explained the significance of this announcement:

- Because of the vital importance of the rule of law to the effectiveness and legitimacy of our national security policy, the Administration is announcing our support for two important components of the international legal framework that covers armed conflicts: Additional Protocol II and Article 75 of Additional Protocol I to the 1949 Geneva Conventions. Additional Protocol II, which contains detailed humane treatment standards and fair trial guarantees that apply in the context of non-international armed conflicts, was originally submitted to the Senate for approval by President Reagan in 1987. The Administration urges the Senate to act as soon as practicable on this Protocol, to which 165 States are party. An extensive interagency review concluded that U.S. military practice is already consistent with the Protocol's provisions. Joining the treaty would not only assist us in continuing to exercise leadership in the international community in developing the law of armed conflict, but would also allow us to reaffirm our commitment to humane treatment in, and compliance with legal standards for, the conduct of armed conflict.

- Article 75 of Additional Protocol I, which sets forth fundamental guarantees for persons in the hands of opposing forces in an international armed conflict, is similarly important to the international legal framework. Although the Administration continues to have significant concerns with Additional Protocol I, Article 75 is a provision of the treaty that is consistent with our current policies and practice and is one that the United States has historically supported.

- Our adherence to these principles is also an important safeguard against the mistreatment of captured U.S. military personnel. The U.S. Government will therefore choose out of a sense of legal obligation to treat the principles set forth in Article 75 as applicable to any individual it detains in an international armed conflict, and expects all other nations to adhere to these principles as well.

29.   The full text of the White House fact sheet is available at www.whitehouse.gov/sites/default/files/Fact_Sheet_--_Guantanamo_and_Detainee_Policy.pdf.

30.   Additionally, in E.O. 13567, issued March 7, 2011, President Obama established a new periodic status review process for detainees at Guantanamo, as discussed in response to Question 8(c). Please also see information pertaining to review of detention in Afghanistan (Question 5(c)), habeas corpus review (Question 8(c)), and conditions at Guantanamo (Question 38).

Response to issues raised in Question 5(c).

31. As stated above, E.O. 13491 requires that all agencies of the U.S. government provide the ICRC with notification of, and timely access to, any individual detained in any armed conflict in the custody or under the effective control of an officer, employee, or other agent of the U.S. government or detained within a facility owned, operated, or controlled by a department or agency of the U.S. government, consistent with DoD regulations and policies. Partnering with the ICRC, DoD has greatly expanded the contact detainees have with their families while in detention. Detainees are given the opportunity to send and receive letters, facilitated by the ICRC, and many of them are able to talk to their families via phone or video teleconference. DoD provides the ICRC ongoing access to individuals detained in armed conflict throughout the duration of their detention.

32. All detainees held by DoD are treated in a manner consistent with U.S. obligations under international and domestic law. Upon arrival in any DoD detention facility, all detainees receive medical screening and any necessary medical treatment. The medical care detainees receive throughout their time in U.S. custody is generally comparable to that which is available to U.S. personnel serving in the same location.

33. The extensive U.S. procedural protections, including rigorous review procedures afforded to law of war detainees in its custody in Afghanistan, as well as litigation establishing that U.S. constitutional habeas corpus jurisdiction does not extend to aliens held in law of war detention in the Bagram detention facility in Afghanistan, are discussed in the 2011 ICCPR Report ¶¶ 520 and 216, incorporated herein by reference. Further, control of the detention facility was transferred to Afghanistan on March 25, 2013, at which time the United States also transferred custody of all Afghan detainees in the facility to Afghan authorities. The facility was renamed the Afghan National Detention Facility-Parwan (ANDF-P).

34. As discussed further in response to Question 8(c), U.S. constitutional habeas corpus jurisdiction has been held to extend to those detained outside the United States in some situations.

35.   The United States does not detain any persons on Diego Garcia. As indicated above in response to Question 5(a), the United States does not have and has never had a detention facility on Diego Garcia.

6. Please indicate what specific measures have been taken to ensure that the State party is fulfilling its international responsibility under the Convention during its intelligence activities, notwithstanding the author, nature or location of those activities.

36.   As noted in response to Question 3, under U.S. law every U.S. official, wherever he or she may be, is prohibited from engaging in torture or in cruel, inhuman or degrading treatment or punishment, at all times, and in all places.

37.   E.O. 13491 provided that all executive directives, orders, and regulations inconsistent with E.O. 13491, including but not limited to those issued to or by the CIA from September 11, 2001 to January 20, 2009 concerning detention or the interrogation of detained individuals, were revoked to the extent of their inconsistency with that order. The DOJ Office of Legal Counsel revoked other prior interpretations of U.S. obligations under, inter alia, the CAT, in the spring of 2009.

38.   The Special Interagency Task Force on Interrogation and Transfer Policies (Special Task Force) established by E.O. 13491 specifically concluded that the Army Field Manual provides appropriate guidance on interrogation for military interrogators, and that no additional or different guidance was necessary for other agencies, including intelligence agencies. For further relevant information, please see response to Question 18.

7. Please indicate if the State party has adopted legal provisions to implement the principle of absolute prohibition of torture in its domestic law without any possible derogation, as recommended by the Committee in its previous concluding observations (para. 19).

39.   The prohibition on torture under U.S. law is absolute, as discussed in response to Question 3. Under U.S. law, every U.S. official, wherever he or she may be, is prohibited from engaging in torture or in cruel, inhuman or degrading treatment or punishment, at all times. Under U.S. law, no exceptional circumstances may be invoked as a justification for torture. Likewise, an order from a superior officer or a public authority may not be invoked as a justification for torture.

8. Please provide updated information on practical steps taken to close down Guantánamo Bay. In this respect, please provide detailed information on:

(a) States which have agreed to accept Guantánamo detainees and which conditions they have imposed. Please elaborate on steps taken to ensure that they are not returned to any State where they could face a real risk of being tortured and guarantee effective post-return monitoring arrangements.

(b) Steps taken to bring to justice those still detained at Guantánamo Bay for crimes under criminal law in regularly constituted courts, in accordance with internationally recognized fair trial standards. Please indicate before which judicial authority such detainees are tried and the legal safeguards with which they are provided.

(c) Steps taken to ensure that the State party will not indefinitely detain suspects, including those currently held at Guantánamo Bay, without charge. In case of such prolonged detention without trial, please elaborate on the legal safeguards provided to the detainees. Do they have the right to access to a lawyer of their own choice?

(d) Measures taken to ensure that all detainees who were kept in detention at Guantánamo Bay can have an enforceable right to fair and adequate compensation, in addition to rehabilitation, if a victim of torture or ill-treatment.

40. The President has repeatedly reaffirmed his commitment to close the Guantanamo detention facility. In his May 23, 2013 speech at the National Defense University, he outlined a series of steps that have been or will be taken to reach this goal, including calling on Congress to lift the restrictions on detainee transfers from Guantanamo; asking DoD to designate a site in the United States where military commissions can be held; appointing new senior envoys at DOS and DoD who will be responsible for negotiating the transfer of detainees; and lifting the moratorium on detainee transfers to Yemen. A fact sheet summarizing the President's speech is available at www.whitehouse.gov/the-press-office/2013/05/23/fact-sheet-president-s-may-23-speech-counterterrorism.

41. The United States derives its domestic authority to detain the individuals at Guantanamo from the 2001 Authorization for Use of Military Force (AUMF), as informed by the laws of war, and as such may detain, inter alia, "persons who were part of, or substantially supported, Taliban or al-Qaeda forces or associated forces that are engaged in hostilities against the United States or coalition partners." Such detention is permitted by the law of war until the cessation of hostilities covered by the AUMF.

42. On January 22, 2009, President Obama issued E.O. 13492, "Review and Disposition of Individuals Detained at the Guantanamo Bay Naval Base and Closure of Detention Facilities,"

15

calling for the closure of the Guantanamo facility. As the President explained, he knew when he ordered Guantanamo closed that the process would be "difficult and complex." This remains true today. But, consistent with its policies and its values, the United States continues to work through these challenging issues in order to close the facility.

43.   Pursuant to E.O. 13492, the United States established a Guantanamo Review Task Force (Task Force) to carry out the review of the status of all detainees then held at Guantanamo. The Task Force, comprised of representatives of DOJ, DoD, DOS and DHS, and of the Office of the Director of National Intelligence and the Joint Chiefs of Staff, painstakingly considered all relevant information in the possession of the U.S. government about each Guantanamo detainee to assess whether it was possible to transfer each individual detained at Guantanamo to his home country or to a third country; or whether he should be referred for prosecution or continue to be held pursuant to the AUMF, as informed by the laws of war. E.O. 13492 and subsequent developments are discussed below.

Response to issues raised in Question 8(a).
44.   On January 22, 2010, the Task Force completed the thorough, rigorous, and collaborative interagency review of the status of 240 individuals then detained at Guantanamo and subject to E.O. 13492. As a result of that process, 126 individuals at Guantanamo were designated for transfer subject to appropriate security measures, 36 detainees were referred for potential prosecution, and 48 detainees were designated for continued law of war detention. In addition, 30 Yemeni national detainees were designated for "conditional detention," meaning that they may be transferred if (1) the security situation improves in Yemen; (2) an appropriate rehabilitation program becomes available; or (3) an appropriate third-country resettlement option becomes available. The Task Force report is available at www.justice.gov/ag/guantanamo-review-final-report.pdf.

45.   Since President Obama took office in 2009, 71 detainees have been transferred to 28 different destinations, including the transfer of 42 detainees to third countries. One detainee, Ahmed Ghailani, was transferred to the custody of the United States Marshals Service for prosecution in the United States District Court for the Southern District of New York, one detainee died of natural causes and three detainees committed suicide. One hundred sixty-six detainees remain at Guantanamo.

46.   Since 2002, more than 600 detainees have departed Guantanamo for other countries, including: Albania, Algeria, Afghanistan, Australia, Bangladesh, Bahrain, Belgium, Bermuda, Bulgaria, Canada, Cape Verde, Chad, Denmark, Egypt, El Salvador, France, Germany, Hungary, Iran, Iraq, Ireland, Italy, Jordan, Kuwait, Latvia, Libya, Maldives, Mauritania, Morocco, Pakistan, Palau, Portugal, Russia, Saudi Arabia, Slovakia, Somalia, Spain, Sweden, Switzerland, Sudan, Tajikistan, Turkey, Uganda, United Kingdom and Yemen.

47.   In a March 7, 2011 statement announcing the issuance of E.O. 13567, the White House reaffirmed the key role of other countries in the process of closing Guantanamo, stating:

> We are grateful to all of our allies and partners who have worked with the Administration to implement the transfers undertaken thus far in a secure and humane manner, especially those who have resettled detainees from third countries. Our friends and allies should know that we remain determined in our efforts and that, with their continued assistance, we intend to complete the difficult challenge of closing Guantanamo.

48.   A core component of U.S. transfer policy is the United States' longstanding and firm commitment not to transfer any detainee from Guantanamo to a State where it is more likely than not that he will be tortured. In Guantanamo transfer cases, especially when detention as a result of a judicial proceeding or other lawful authority by the receiving country is foreseen, the U.S. government seeks assurances of humane treatment, including treatment in accordance with the international obligations of the destination country. In every decision to transfer a detainee, the U.S. government takes into account the totality of relevant factors relating to the individual and the government in question, including but not limited to any assurances that have been provided. As indicated in response to Questions 8(c), the Secretary of State is involved in obtaining and evaluating diplomatic assurances in all transfers.

49.   When evaluating the adequacy of any treatment assurances, U.S. officials consider, inter alia, the foreign government's past practice and capacity to fulfill its assurances, relevant political or legal developments in the foreign country concerned, and U.S. diplomatic relations with that country. There have been 58 detainee transfers from Guantanamo to other countries since the Special Task Force established under E.O. 13491 issued its recommendations on

treatment assurances in the transfer of detainees by the United States, as discussed in response to Question 11(a). As part of obtaining treatment assurances in these transfers, the United States has also sought, where applicable, to secure access for post-transfer humanitarian monitoring by credible, independent organizations capable of conducting such monitoring. In instances in which the United States transfers an individual subject to assurances, it would pursue any credible report of conduct contrary to those assurances and take appropriate action – including possible corrective steps – if it had reason to believe that those assurances would not be, or had not been, honored. Where specific concerns about treatment could not be resolved satisfactorily, the United States has declined to transfer the individual to the country of concern.

Response to issues raised in Question 8(b).

50.   In response to the Supreme Court's decision in Hamdan v. Rumsfeld, 548 U.S. 557 (2006), which invalidated then-existing military commissions, Congress passed the 2006 Military Commissions Act, 120 Stat. 2600 (MCA 2006), authorizing the use of military commissions by the Executive Branch.

51.   The Military Commissions Act of 2009 (MCA 2009), enacted in October 2009, made many significant changes to the system of military commissions, including: prohibiting the admission at trial of statements obtained by use of torture or cruel, inhuman, or degrading treatment, except against a person accused of torture or such treatment as evidence that the statement was made; strengthening the restrictions on admission of hearsay evidence; stipulating that an accused in a capital case be provided with counsel "learned in applicable law relating to capital cases;" providing the accused with greater latitude in selecting his or her own military defense counsel; enhancing the accused's right to discovery; and establishing new procedures for handling classified information. The MCA 2009 also provides for review of final judgments by the U.S. Court of Appeals for the District of Columbia Circuit, as further described below.

52.   In a military commission convened under Chapter 47A of Title 10 U.S.C., as amended by the MCA 2009, prosecution may not commence until an impartial convening authority makes the independent decision to refer charges, sworn by a prosecutor, to a military commission. The military commission comprises a panel of impartial military officers who are examined under oath for suitability by the impartial judge presiding over the military commission, as well as by the prosecution and defense. Any attempt to influence the military commission, convening

authority, prosecutors, or defense counsel by unauthorized means is prohibited. If an accused is convicted and sentenced by the military commission, the conviction and sentence must be reviewed and approved by the convening authority. If the conviction and sentence are approved by the convening authority and the accused does not waive his appellate rights (appellate rights may not be waived in capital cases), then the conviction and sentence will automatically be reviewed by the U.S. Court of Military Commission Review. The accused may also petition the D.C. Circuit Court of Appeals for review of a final judgment rendered by a military commission (as approved by the convening authority and, where applicable, the U.S. Court of Military Commission Review), and then may petition the Supreme Court for review of the final D.C. Circuit Court of Appeals judgment.

53.   An individual tried before a military commission enjoys many rights in addition to those under the MCA 2009 enumerated above, including but not limited to: notice of the allegations against him, defense counsel (at no cost), the requirement that the presumption of innocence be overcome by proof beyond a reasonable doubt, the right to be present during trial, the right to obtain evidence and witnesses, the right to respond to the government's evidence and witnesses, and the prohibition against compulsory self-incrimination.

54.   Military commissions convicted three detainees under the MCA 2006. David Hicks was convicted of material support for terrorism and sentenced to seven years confinement. His sentence was reduced via a pre-trial agreement to 9 months confinement at Guantanamo with the remainder served in his native Australia. Salim Hamdan was convicted of material support for terrorism and acquitted of conspiracy; he was sentenced to five and a half years confinement. His sentence was reduced by five years and one month on account of pre-trial confinement, and he has since been transferred to Yemen and released. Ali Hamza al-Bahlul was convicted of conspiracy, solicitation, and providing material support for terrorism and sentenced to confinement for life. The Hamdan and Bahlul convictions were vacated by the D.C. Circuit Court of Appeals in October 2012 and January 2013, respectively, although the court has since granted the government's petition for rehearing en banc in Bahlul's case, and has scheduled oral argument to be held September 30, 2013.

55.   Since the enactment of the MCA 2009, there have been four convictions: Ibrahim al Qosi pleaded guilty to conspiracy and providing material support for terrorism; Mr. al Qosi has since been repatriated to Sudan. Omar Khadr pleaded guilty to murder in violation of the law of war, attempted murder in violation of the law of war, conspiracy, providing material support for terrorism, and spying; Mr. Khadr has been repatriated to Canada to serve the remainder of his sentence. Noor Uthman Muhammed pleaded guilty to charges of conspiracy and providing material support to al-Qaeda. In February 2012 Majid Khan pleaded guilty to five charges.

56.   On April 4, 2012, the United States referred to a military commission charges against Khalid Sheikh Mohammed and his four alleged co-conspirators in the September 11 attacks. Pre-trial proceedings are currently underway.

57.   In a fact sheet issued on March 7, 2011, the White House detailed the continuing commitment of the United States to trials in its courts. A White House Fact Sheet describing this commitment is available at: www.whitehouse.gov/sites/default/files/Fact_Sheet_--_Guantanamo_and_Detainee_Policy.pdf. On May 23, 2013, the President reiterated that, "where appropriate, we will bring terrorists to justice in our courts." Additionally, the President announced that he had asked DoD to designate a site in the United States where military commissions can be held.

58.   In signing the National Defense Authorization Act (NDAA) for Fiscal Year 2013, Public Law 112-239, on January 2, 2013, President Obama objected to restrictions contained in the statute on using appropriated funds for fiscal year 2013 to transfer Guantanamo detainees into the United States for any purpose, including trial, and to unwarranted restrictions on executive branch authority to transfer detainees to foreign countries. The President stated that these provisions would, under certain circumstances, violate constitutional separation of powers principles, and that his Administration will interpret them to avoid constitutional conflict. President Obama objected to the same restrictions in signing the NDAA for fiscal years 2011 and 2012.

Response to issues raised in Question 8(c).
59.   The individuals detained at Guantanamo pursuant to the 2001 AUMF, as informed by the laws of war, are detained as "persons who were part of, or substantially supported, Taliban or al-

Qaeda forces or associated forces that are engaged in hostilities against the United States or coalition partners."

60.   Pursuant to the decision in <u>Boumediene v. Bush</u>, 553 U.S. 723 (2008) (upholding constitutional habeas corpus jurisdiction over claims of aliens detained at Guantanamo), detainees have continued to challenge the legality of their detention via habeas corpus petitions in the U.S. federal district court in the District of Columbia, with a right of appeal to the D.C. Circuit Court of Appeals. These courts are part of the independent judicial branch of the U.S. government, and are separate from the Executive Branch (which includes the military). Each detainee held by the United States in law of war detention at Guantanamo is entitled to petition the U.S. federal courts for habeas corpus review of the lawfulness of his detention. Many Guantanamo detainees have availed themselves of this right, and the district and appellate courts have completed their review of approximately 50 habeas cases to date. All of the detainees who have prevailed in habeas proceedings under orders that are no longer subject to appeal have either been repatriated or resettled, or have received offers of resettlement. Approximately 14 detainees have been released after winning their habeas cases in federal courts.

61.   The federal courts have worked to ensure appropriate process and protections for these proceedings. Detainees have access to counsel of their choice and to appropriate evidence, and are assured a means of challenging the lawfulness of their detention before an independent court. Except in the rare instances where required by compelling security interests, all of the evidence relied upon by the government to justify detention in habeas proceedings is disclosed to the detainees' counsel, who have been granted security clearances to view the classified evidence. The detainees may submit written statements and provide live testimony at their hearings via video link. The United States has the burden in these cases to establish its legal authority to hold the detainees.

62.   On March 7, 2011, President Obama issued E.O. 13567 establishing a new regime of periodic review for the detainees at the Guantanamo detention facility who have not been charged, convicted, or designated for transfer. The E.O. provides for an initial review of each detainee subject to the review process before an interagency Periodic Review Board (PRB), which is composed of representatives of the Departments of State, Defense, Justice, and

Homeland Security and the Offices of the Director of National Intelligence and the Chairman of the Joint Chiefs of Staff. The PRB is charged with determining whether continued law of war detention of a detainee subject to the periodic review process is necessary to protect against a significant threat to the security of the United States. If a final determination is made that a detainee no longer constitutes a significant threat to U.S. national security requiring his continued detention, the E.O. provides that the Secretaries of State and Defense are to ensure that vigorous efforts are undertaken to identify a suitable transfer location outside the United States, consistent with the national security and foreign policy interests of the United States and the commitment of the United States not to transfer any person to a country where it is more likely than not that the person will be tortured. The E.O. also expressly provides that the periodic review process must be implemented "consistent with applicable law including: the Convention Against Torture; Common Article 3 of the Geneva Conventions; the Detainee Treatment Act of 2005; and other laws relating to the transfer, treatment, and interrogation of individuals detained in an armed conflict." On July 19, 2013, the Department of Defense notified private counsel for certain detainees of the commencement of the periodic review process. The E.O. also makes the Secretary of State, in consultation with the Secretary of Defense, responsible for obtaining appropriate security and humane treatment assurances regarding any detainee to be transferred to another country.

Response to issues raised in Question 8(d).
63.   E.O. 13492 requires that "[n]o individual currently detained at Guantanamo shall be held in the custody or under the effective control of any officer, employee, or other agent of the United States Government, or at a facility owned, operated, or controlled by a department or agency of the United States, except in conformity with all applicable laws governing the conditions of such confinement, including Common Article 3 of the Geneva Conventions." This E.O. directed the Secretary of Defense to undertake a comprehensive review of the conditions of confinement at Guantanamo to assess compliance with its directive. The review concluded in February 2009 that operations at Guantanamo were "in conformity with all applicable laws governing the conditions of confinement, including Common Article 3 of the Geneva Conventions." The review team noted "that the chain of command responsible for the detention mission at Guantanamo seeks to go beyond a minimalist approach to compliance with Common Article 3, and endeavors to enhance conditions in a manner as humane as possible consistent

with security concerns." The report is available at

www.defense.gov/pubs/pdfs/REVIEW_OF_DEPARTMENT_COMPLIANCE_WITH_PRESID
ENTS_EXECUTIVE_ORDER_ON_DETAINEE_CONDITIONS_OF_CONFINEMENTa.pdf.

Additional information concerning conditions of detention at Guantanamo is provided in

response to Question 38. Claims based on allegations of torture or ill-treatment are discussed in

response to Question 27.

9. Please describe steps taken to ensure that the Material Witness Statute and immigration laws are not used so as to detain persons suspected of terrorism or any other criminal offences with fewer guarantees than in criminal proceedings.

64.   Federal law permits detention of a person to secure his or her presence as a

material witness at an upcoming trial, see 18 U.S.C. 3144, or for a grand jury. Material

witnesses enjoy the same constitutional right to pretrial release as other federal detainees,

and federal law requires release if their testimony "can adequately be secured by

deposition, and if further detention is not necessary to prevent a failure of justice." 18

U.S.C. 3144. U.S. law concerning detention for this purpose is discussed in the 2011

ICCPR Report ¶ 211, incorporated herein by reference.

65.   DHS does not use the Material Witness Statute to detain individuals in immigration

removal proceedings. Every individual in DHS custody pending removal proceedings is provided

with an "opportunity to be heard," see Mathews v. Eldridge, 424 U.S. 319, 333 (1976), in those

proceedings and generally may request release on bond pursuant to 8 U.S.C. 1226(a), unless the

alien has committed an offense or offenses that render the alien's detention mandatory under 8

U.S.C. 1226(c), or parole under 8 U.S.C. 1182(d)(5). The U.S. Supreme Court has upheld such

pre-removal detention as constitutional. See Demore v. Kim, 538 U.S. 510 (2003). Aliens subject

to mandatory detention under the immigration laws, may, however, file petitions for writs of

habeas corpus to challenge the legality of their detention. In addition, an alien may challenge in a

hearing before an immigration judge the propriety of his or her inclusion in the category of aliens

subject to mandatory detention under 8 U.S.C. 1226(c). 8 C.F.R. 1003.19(h)(2)(ii). Although 8

U.S.C. 1226a provides for immigration detention of suspected alien terrorists under certain

circumstances, that authority has never been exercised. Once an alien has been ordered removed

from the United States, detention is mandatory for a 90-day period pending removal for most criminal aliens and those who pose a national security risk. 8 U.S.C. 1231(a)(1)-(2). The U.S. Supreme Court has indicated that a period of detention of up to six months after an order of removal becomes administratively final is presumptively reasonable for the United States to accomplish an alien's removal. Zadvydas v. Davis, 533 U.S. 678 (2001); Clark v. Martinez, 543 U.S. 371 (2005). With limited exceptions (e.g., on national security grounds), after six months the continued detention of an alien ordered removed is no longer presumptively lawful, and the alien must be released under terms of supervision if the alien can show that there is no significant likelihood of removal in the reasonably foreseeable future. DHS codified this standard in implementing regulations published in 8 C.F.R. 241.13-14. Detention and removal of aliens is discussed further in the 2011 ICCPR Report ¶¶ 213-214 and 257-281, incorporated herein by reference.

Article 3

In light of the Committee's previous concluding observations (para. 20), please provide updated information on:

(a) Steps taken to ensure that the State party applies the non-refoulement guarantee to all detainees in its custody, including those detained outside its territory. Please provide information on steps taken to establish adequate judicial mechanisms to challenge all refoulement decisions.

(b) Whether the State party has ceased the "rendition" of suspects, in particular by its intelligence agencies, to States where they face a real risk of torture, as recommended by the Committee in its previous concluding observations.

(c) Steps taken to ensure that the State party conducts investigations into all allegations of violation of article 3 of the Convention. Please elaborate on the outcome of these investigations and the impact thereof on the State party's policy (CCPR/C/USA/CO/3/Rev.1, para. 16).

Response to issues raised in Question 10(a).

66.   Noting paragraph 6 of this Report, United States policy is not to transfer any person to a country where it is more likely than not that the person will be tortured or, in appropriate cases, where the person has a well-founded fear of persecution based on a protected ground and would not be disqualified from persecution protection on criminal or security-related grounds. Section 2242 of the Foreign Affairs Reform and Restructuring Act of 1998, Pub. L. No. 105-277 (FARRA) provides that "[i]t shall be the policy of the United States not to expel, extradite, or otherwise effect the involuntary return of any person to a country in which there are substantial

grounds for believing the person would be in danger of being subjected to torture, regardless of whether the person is physically present in the United States." In application, the "substantial grounds" standard equates to the "more likely than not" standard.[1] The clear statement in the FARRA informs U.S. treatment of detainees in its custody, and others subject to transfer by the United States.

67.   In E.O. 13491, President Obama ordered the establishment of the Special Task Force in part "to study and evaluate the practices of transferring individuals to other nations in order to ensure that such practices comply with the domestic laws, international obligations, and policies of the United States and do not result in the transfer of individuals to other nations to face torture or otherwise for the purpose, or with the effect, of undermining or circumventing the commitments or obligations of the United States to ensure the humane treatment of individuals in its custody or control." The Special Task Force considered seven types of transfers conducted by the U.S. government: extradition, removals pursuant to immigration proceedings, transfers pursuant to the Geneva Conventions, transfers from Guantanamo, military transfers within or from Afghanistan, military transfers within or from Iraq, and transfers pursuant to intelligence authorities. The work of the Special Task Force was informed, inter alia, by the record in past cases. Recommendations made by the Special Task Force in August 2009, were accepted by the President. The Special Task Force was terminated upon the completion of its duties.

68.   The United States maintains extensive mechanisms to ensure that all transfers are conducted in a manner consistent with its non-refoulement commitment, as discussed in response to Questions 8(a) and 11. In its Initial Report ¶¶ 156-177, 2005 CAT Report ¶¶ 32-43, and 2006 Response to List of Issues pp. 27-32, 39-43 and 46, the United States provided detailed information on the implementation of Article 3 in the immigration removal and extradition contexts. See, e.g., DHS regulations for the implementation of Article 3 in the immigration removal context, 8 C.F.R. 208.16-208.18, and DOS regulations implementing Article 3 in the extradition context, 22 C.F.R. 95.1-95.4. U.S. implementation of Article 3 of the Convention in

---

[1] As discussed in previous submissions, in order to clarify the definitional scope of "substantial grounds" in article 3, the United States conditioned its ratification on a formal understanding that the phrase "where there are substantial grounds for believing that he would be in danger of being subjected to torture," means "if it is more likely than not that he would be tortured." See Initial Report ¶ 158, 2005 CAT Report ¶ 30 and 2006 Response to List of Issues pp. 37-38.

the immigration and extradition context is discussed further in the 2011 ICCPR Report ¶¶ 282-287 and ¶¶ 558-559, incorporated herein by reference.

69.   As addressed elsewhere in this submission, the United States conducts a thorough, case-by-case analysis of each potential transfer to a foreign government of third country nationals detained in situations of armed conflict and may secure diplomatic assurances from the country of proposed transfer, as well as post-transfer monitoring of the detainee. This thorough and rigorous process ensures that any transfers are consistent with the U.S. non-refoulement commitment.

70.   The United States also takes measures to ensure that law of war detainees who are transferred to a host government are treated humanely. In Afghanistan, for example, the International Security Assistance Force (ISAF) temporarily suspended detainee transfers to a number of Afghan facilities while examining credible reports of detainee abuse in those facilities. ISAF policy is to transfer detainees only to those facilities that are certified by Commander ISAF as eligible for transfer. This certification determination is based on a number of factors, and could involve inspections, remediation training, implementation of accountability measures, monitoring by ISAF, and efforts to enhance transparency. The facilities eligible for transfer are subject to re-certification on a quarterly basis. ISAF and the U.S. Embassy have also devoted significant resources, including through technical advisers, to increasing the capacity of the Afghan National Security Forces to conduct secure and humane detention operations. The United States has also sought and received assurances from the Government of Afghanistan that transferred detainees will be treated humanely, consistent with Afghanistan's international obligations, and that organizations will have access to all transferred detainees. As indicated in response to Question 5, the transfer of all Afghan detainees held in what was then the Detention Facility in Parwan (DFIP) to Afghanistan was completed on March 25, 2013, and U.S. forces maintain a physical presence at the facility to ensure appropriate treatment of all transferred detainees. The United States continues to hold third country nationals at the ANDF-P and is assessing potential disposition options for those individuals.

Response to issues raised in Question 10(b).

71.   The United States does not transfer any individual to a foreign country if it is more likely than not that the person would be tortured. The Special Task Force established in E.O. 13491 issued a set of recommendations to ensure that U.S. transfer practices comply with the domestic laws, international obligations, and policies of the United States and do not result in the transfer of individuals to other nations to face torture, and the President accepted those recommendations. The U.S. government is in the process of implementing those recommendations.

Response to issues raised in Question 10(c).

72.   The United States is firm in its commitment not to transfer any person to a country where it is more likely than not that the person will be tortured, as discussed further in response to Questions 8 and 11. Assignment of responsibility within the U.S. government for investigating alleged violations of this law and policy necessarily depends on the specific facts and circumstances of the allegations. If criminal violations of federal law are suspected, DOJ may investigate. In other cases, the Inspector General's office or another component of the agency involved may investigate.

73.   Informed in part by the DHS Office of Inspector General's (DHS/OIG) report on the Maher Arar removal matter, which is available in redacted form at www.oig.dhs.gov/assets/Mgmt/OIGr_08-18_Jun08.pdf, the Special Task Force made a series of recommendations on the implementation of Article 3 of the Convention, including consideration of diplomatic assurances in immigration removal proceedings.

74.   In November 2011, DHS/OIG completed a report on DHS practices and regulations implementing Article 3 in the removal context, including a discussion of the process for considering diplomatic assurances in removal cases. This extensive report, including the DHS response, is available in redacted form at www.oig.dhs.gov/assets/Mgmt/OIG_11-100_Nov11.pdf. As recognized in the DHS/OIG report, DHS has established significant procedural safeguards for removal cases in which reliable diplomatic assurances have been obtained by DOS and transmitted to DHS pursuant to law.

75. The United States is not aware of any cases in which humane treatment assurances have not been honored in the case of an individual transferred from the United States or Guantanamo since the Special Task Force report was issued in August 2009.

11. Please provide detailed information on:

(a) The procedures in place for obtaining "diplomatic assurances", as requested by the Committee in its previous concluding observations (para. 21). A reminder to this effect was sent by the Rapporteur for follow-up in his letter of 8 August 2008.
(b) Steps taken to establish a judicial mechanism for reviewing, in last instance, the sufficiency and appropriateness of diplomatic assurances in any applicable case. Please elaborate on the federal court ruling in the case of Sameh Khouzam, noting that "deporting Khouzam based on diplomatic assurances without court review would render the procedures established for seeking protection under the Convention Against Torture "a farce". Please provide information on other cases of this kind, if any.
(c) Steps taken to guarantee effective post-return monitoring arrangements.
(d) All cases since 11 September 2001 where diplomatic assurances have been provided. Furthermore, please indicate if the State party has received information on any assurances that have not been honoured and what appropriate actions were taken in such cases by the State party?

Response to issues raised in Question 11(a).
76. For the United States, the critical determination in the context of any transfer of an individual to a foreign country is whether it is more likely than not that the person would be tortured. U.S. consideration and use of assurances from foreign governments regarding the treatment of people who may be transferred to foreign countries, where such assurances are relevant, factor into this determination.

77. As noted, in August 2009 the Special Task Force made recommendations to the President with respect to all scenarios in which the United States transfers or facilitates the transfer of a person from one country to another or from U.S. custody to the custody of another country. The Special Task Force recommendations were accepted by the President. Several recommendations were aimed at clarifying and strengthening U.S. procedures for obtaining and evaluating diplomatic assurances from receiving countries for those transfers in which such assurances are obtained.[2] These included a recommendation that the Secretary of State be involved in evaluating all diplomatic assurances, and a recommendation that the Inspectors General of the

---

[2] See "Special Task Force on Interrogations and Transfer Policies Issues Its Recommendations to the President," available at www.justice.gov/opa/pr/2009/August/09-ag-835 html (Aug. 24, 2009).

Departments of State, Defense, and Homeland Security prepare annually a coordinated report on all transfers involving diplomatic assurances conducted by each of their agencies. The Special Task Force also made several recommendations aimed at improving U.S. monitoring of the treatment of individuals transferred to other countries pursuant to assurances. In addition, the Special Task Force made recommendations that are specific to military transfer scenarios, and classified recommendations designed to ensure that, in cases where the Intelligence Community participates in or otherwise supports a transfer, affected individuals are provided proper treatment. The United States has been implementing the Special Task Force recommendations across the range of government transfers.

78.   When evaluating the adequacy of treatment assurances provided in any transfer situation, the United States considers a range of factors, as described in response to Question 8(a). If, taking into account all relevant information, including any assurances received, the United States believes that it is more likely than not that a person would be tortured if transferred to a foreign country, the United States would not approve the transfer of the person to that country. There have been cases where the United States has considered the use of diplomatic assurances, but declined to return individuals because the United States was not satisfied such an assurance would satisfy its obligations under its non-refoulement commitment. On the other hand, assurances have been sought in some contexts as a prudential matter, to reduce further any meaningful risk of mistreatment, rather than because they were determined to be necessary for the transfer to be consistent with the U.S. non-refoulement commitment. In cases where diplomatic assurances are sought, the specific parameters are determined on a case-by-case basis.

Response to issues raised in Question 11(b).
79.   A judicial mechanism is generally not available to review diplomatic assurances regarding humane treatment. That said, the United States maintains robust procedures to review the sufficiency and appropriateness of humane treatment assurances, which are different in nature from formal judicial review but effective in ensuring compliance with applicable law and policy. The Executive Branch, and in particular DOS, has the tools to obtain and evaluate assurances of humane treatment, to make recommendations about whether transfers can be made consistent with U.S. government policy on humane treatment, and where appropriate to follow up with receiving governments on compliance with those assurances. DOS has used these tools

in the past to facilitate transfers in a responsible manner that comports with the obligations and policies described herein.

80.   Procedural protections for immigration removal and extradition proceedings related to diplomatic assurances are discussed further in the 2011 ICCPR Report ¶¶ 557 (including discussion of <u>Khouzam</u>) and 559, incorporated herein by reference.

81.   In the law of war context, as elsewhere, DOS's ability to seek and obtain assurances from a foreign government depends in part on the ability to treat its dealings with the foreign government with discretion. This is especially true in the case of detainees at Guantanamo Bay. Consistent with the diplomatic sensitivities that surround DOS communications with foreign governments concerning such law of war detainees, DOS does not make public the specific assurances or other precautionary measures obtained. DOS disclosure outside appropriate Executive Branch channels of its communications with a foreign government regarding the unique matters often involved in detainee transfers could undermine the ability to reach acceptable accommodations with the same or other governments to address important concerns. U.S. federal courts have found that it is for the political branches, not the judiciary, to address concerns raised in circumstances in which the United States had affirmed its compliance with its firm commitment not to transfer individuals to countries where it is more likely than not that they will be tortured. <u>See</u> <u>Munaf v. Geren</u>, 553 U.S. 674, 702 (2008) (holding that the "Judiciary is not suited to second-guess such determinations – determinations that would require federal courts to pass judgment on foreign justice systems and undermine the Government's ability to speak with one voice in this area").

Response to issues raised in Question 11(c).

82.   Consistent with the recommendations of the Special Task Force established under E.O. 13491, in general, the U.S. government will seek the foreign government's agreement to allow consistent, private access to the individual who has been transferred, with minimal advance notice to the detaining government, by non-governmental entities, or in some circumstances U.S. government officials, in the country concerned to monitor the condition of an individual returned to that country. In the past several years, the United States has established monitoring regimes in particular cases. In appropriate situations, the United States has raised concerns regarding both

treatment and the process under which prosecutions have been pursued post-transfer when concerns have been brought to its attention, whether from U.S. government information, monitoring by non-governmental organizations, or other sources. The United States has also taken other measures, such as training guard forces in anticipation of transfers, and has suspended transfers, where appropriate.

Response to issues raised in Question 11(d).

83.   As discussed above, diplomatic assurances have been sought and obtained from foreign governments in an extremely small number of immigration and extradition cases, sometimes as a prudential matter. In an effort to maintain the ability to manage the delicate negotiations needed to obtain assurances, the United States does not as a general matter publicly release the names of countries from which it has secured assurances.

84.   In the law of war detention context, the U.S. government has in many cases obtained humane treatment assurances along with security-related assurances. As explained in the response to Question 11(b), the United States is not in a position to provide further detail on such cases, but U.S. practices in this area are fully consistent with U.S. humane treatment commitments. In Afghanistan, the United States sought and received assurances of humane treatment and access for humanitarian monitoring on multiple occasions – including prior to transferring the remaining Afghan detainees at the DFIP to Afghan authorities in March 2013 – and routinely monitors facilities where transferred detainees are located. In appropriate cases the United States has sought and received humane treatment assurances prior to transferring third country nationals at the DFIP out of Afghanistan. With respect to detainee transfers from U.S. facilities in Iraq to the Iraqi authorities, in certain instances where U.S. military commanders or judge advocates determined that it was necessary, they requested and received specific humane treatment assurances from relevant Iraqi authorities. The United States also sought and received general humane treatment and access assurances in 2011 with respect to transferring detainees from U.S. facilities in Iraq to the Iraqi authorities. Assurances concerning transfers from Guantanamo are discussed in response to Question 8(a).

85.   In instances in which the United States transfers an individual subject to diplomatic assurances, it would pursue any credible report of conduct contrary to those assurances and take appropriate action if it had reason to believe that those assurances would not be, or had not been,

31

honored. The United States takes seriously past practice by foreign governments. In an instance in which specific concerns about the treatment an individual may receive in a particular country cannot be resolved satisfactorily, the United States would seek alternative arrangements. The United States has declined to transfer based on prior failure to comply with humane treatment commitments.

12. Please provide updated information on the security agreement reached between the State Party and Iraq on the transfer of detainees held by the State party to Iraqi custody and the safeguards included to ensure that detainees are not in danger of being tortured. Does each detainee have the opportunity to contest a transfer to Iraqi custody?

86.   Consistent with its terms, the Agreement Between the United States of America and the Republic of Iraq on the Withdrawal of United States Forces from Iraq and the Organization of their Activities During Their Temporary Presence in Iraq (Security Agreement) expired on December 31, 2011. All detainees in U.S. physical custody were released or transferred to the Ministry of Justice of the Government of Iraq prior to the expiration of the agreement. The U.S. government sought and received assurances from the Government of Iraq that Iraq was committed to treating detainees in accordance with its Constitution and its international human rights obligations, including the CAT.

87.   During the period in which the United States was involved in holding detainees in Iraq on behalf of the Iraqi government, the U.S. Supreme Court held that habeas corpus jurisdiction could not be exercised to enjoin the United States from transferring a U.S. citizen to the custody of Iraq, a foreign sovereign, for criminal trial where the individuals were detained within its territory on behalf of that sovereign pending their criminal prosecution, and where the U.S. government had a firm policy not to transfer individuals if they were more likely than not to face torture. Munaf v. Geren, 553 U.S. 674 (2008). Nevertheless, the United States took appropriate action, before and after the Security Agreement went into effect, to mitigate the risk that any transferred detainees would be subject to torture.

88.   As part of this effort, DOS has implemented extensive training and assistance programs for Iraqi prisons. Since 2003, more than 15,000 Iraqi correctional officers have received training through DOS programs. The United States has also helped the Iraqis establish their own training and auditing programs to promote and protect human rights, and has provided improved facilities

and ongoing partnering. Although all U.S. forces have now withdrawn from Iraq, the United States continues its partnership with Iraq through DOS programs such as these, as well as through regular bilateral dialogue regarding detention and treatment issues.

Articles 5 and 7

13. Please indicate whether the State party has rejected, for any reason, any request for extradition by another State of an individual suspected of having committed an offence of torture and started its own prosecution proceedings as a result since the consideration of the previous report. If so, please provide information on the status and outcome of such proceedings.

89.   The United States has not rejected any request for extradition of an individual certified extraditable for committing a torture offense since its last submission to the Committee in 2006.

14. Please indicate what are the purposes of the agreements the State party is signing with countries not to transfer its citizens to the International Criminal Court to be prosecuted for war crimes or crimes against humanity and how does the State party ensure that this combats impunity? Please provide examples of such cases, if any. With how many States has the State party signed such agreements? Should these agreements prove not to be effective in combating impunity, please provide information on any other measures taken by the State party to combat impunity in such cases.

90.   The United States has signed agreements with over 100 States of the type described above that apply to United States persons. In general, States concluding the agreements agree to surrender or transfer such persons to the International Criminal Court only with the consent of the State concerned. To date there have not been any requests for such consent under these agreements. For its part, the United States is fully committed to investigating and prosecuting, where appropriate, acts that amount to war crimes, crimes against humanity, and genocide alleged to have been committed by its officials, employees, military personnel or other nationals. Indeed, the agreements contain language specifically underscoring this intention, and reaffirming the importance of bringing to justice those who commit war crimes, crimes against humanity, and genocide, and this would include any such crimes that are covered by the CAT.

15. Please provide information on any judicial cooperation between the State party and Colombia regarding Colombian paramilitary leaders who were extradited to the State party and their responsibility for gross human rights violations, in order to ensure the prosecution of the perpetrators and satisfy the right to justice, truth and compensation of the victims.

Response to issues raised in Question 15.

91.   The United States has committed that it will take reasonable steps to facilitate access by Colombian prosecutors, judges, and other criminal justice officials to former Colombian paramilitary leaders incarcerated in U.S. jails, consistent with applicable international conventions and practices and the interest of the criminal prosecutions in the United States. Fourteen of the individuals currently incarcerated in the United States were extradited from Colombia in May 2008 on the order of then-President Alvaro Uribe, finding that the individuals were not complying with the terms of the Colombian Justice and Peace Law (Law 975 of 2005), under which they had received reduced prison terms in exchange for confessions of their crimes and compensation for their victims. The extradition of a number of significant paramilitary leaders to the United States in 2008 necessitated the institution of procedures to ensure Colombian officials could maintain access to the extradited paramilitary leaders to continue investigating human rights abuses that these individuals may have instigated.

92.   To simplify the transmission of judicial assistance requests regarding those former paramilitaries, the U.S. Embassy in Bogota agreed to receive and forward to DOJ, Office of International Affairs, all judicial assistance requests related to the former paramilitary leaders extradited to the United States in May 2008 and thereafter. These procedures have worked extremely well to facilitate interviews and video sessions for both the former United Self-Defense Forces of Colombia (Unidas de Colombia or AUC) and Revolutionary Armed Forces of Colombia (Fuerzas Armadas Revolucionarias de Colombia or FARC) defendants. Pursuant to Colombian judicial assistance requests made under the Organization of American States mutual legal assistance convention regarding the former paramilitary leaders, DOJ has facilitated more than 500 video depositions and interviews, which occur daily, five days a week, from three U.S. facilities (Virginia, Miami, and New York). These include video depositions in Colombian criminal cases pending before the Supreme Court of Justice and investigations under the Justice and Peace Law. These proceedings, many of which were transmitted to victims throughout Colombia, have advanced numerous prosecutions and investigations of individuals in Colombia, as well as the identification and forfeiture of substantial assets.

93.   In addition, a number of other Colombian officials who are not accredited consular officers, prosecutors, or criminal justice officials covered by the mutual legal assistance treaty

have also been given access to several former paramilitary leaders. These officials include members of the Colombian legislature, who have stated their intention and desire to advance the Justice and Peace process by seeking the former paramilitaries' continued cooperation in providing information about their human rights violations and abuses and providing restitution to victims and their survivors.

Article 10

16. Please include information on steps taken to:

(a) **Ensure that education and training of all law enforcement or military personnel is conducted on a regular basis, in particular for personnel involved in the interrogation of suspects. Does this include training on interrogation rules, instructions and methods, as well as specific training on how to identify signs of torture and cruel, inhuman or degrading treatment? Are personnel instructed to report such incidents?**
(b) **Ensure specific training for all medical personnel dealing with detainees in the detection of signs of torture and ill-treatment and ensure that the Istanbul Protocol of 1999 becomes an integral part of the training provided to physicians and others involved in care of detainees.**
(c) **Develop and implement a methodology to evaluate the implementation of its training/educational programmes, and their effectiveness and impact on the reduction of cases of torture and ill-treatment. Please provide information on the content and implementation of such methodology, as well as on the results of the measures implemented.**

Response to issues raised in Question 16(a).

94.   DoD intelligence interrogations are conducted only by properly trained and certified personnel. Training includes instruction on applicable law and policy; lawful interrogation methods and techniques; the humane treatment of detainees and how to identify signs of torture and/or cruel, inhuman or degrading treatment; and the procedures for the reporting of alleged violations. Routine refresher training is provided on a recurring basis. Refresher training is also provided by Combatant Commanders to all interrogators when they are assigned to conduct operations in a specific theater.

95.   Under DoD Directive 3115.09 (DoD Intelligence Interrogations, Detainee Debriefings, and Tactical Questioning, October 11, 2012), alleged violations by any DoD personnel or DoD contractor personnel must be promptly reported in accordance with specific guidelines, promptly and thoroughly investigated by proper authorities, and remedied by disciplinary or administrative

action, when appropriate. On-scene commanders and supervisors are instructed to ensure measures are taken to preserve evidence pertaining to any reportable incident. Reportable incidents allegedly committed by non-DoD U.S. or foreign personnel are required to be reported to proper authorities for appropriate action. The Directive defines "reportable incident" as "[a]ny suspected or alleged violation of DoD policy, procedures, or applicable law relating to intelligence interrogations, detainee debriefings, or tactical questioning for which there is credible information."

96.   The Federal Bureau of Investigation (FBI) uses a non-coercive rapport-based approach to interrogation, and FBI policy specifically prohibits the use of force, threats, or promises in the course of an interrogation. Although the FBI instructs its agents on the elements of effective interrogation, it does not define a particular set of techniques for its agents to use. All FBI Special Agents receive extensive training on interview and interrogation during their new agents training classes in Quantico, Virginia. Training is conducted in the classroom and through practical exercises. FBI personnel may attend additional interrogation training after basic training.

97.   Specific FBI policies on interrogation covered by this training include:

- According to longstanding FBI policy and practice and consistent with E.O. 13491, FBI personnel must treat all suspects humanely.
- No interrogation shall be conducted using methods that could be interpreted as inherently coercive, such as physical abuse or threat of such abuse to the persons being interrogated or to any third party, or imposing severe physical conditions.
- FBI personnel shall not participate in any treatment or use any interrogation technique that is in violation of FBI guidelines regardless of whether the co-interrogator is in compliance with his or her own guidelines.
- If a co-interrogator is complying with rules of his/her agency, but the conduct is not in compliance with FBI rules, FBI personnel may not participate in the interrogation and must remove themselves from the situation.

In addition, if an FBI employee knows of or suspects any abuse or mistreatment of a detainee, the FBI employee must report the incident to the FBI on-scene Commander, who reports the information to FBI headquarters. FBI headquarters is responsible for further follow-up.

98.   Inmates in federal prison may be questioned in relation to ongoing criminal or administrative investigations by Bureau of Prisons (BOP) employees. BOP policy states that "An employee may not use brutality, physical violence, or intimidation toward inmates, or use any force beyond that which is reasonably necessary to subdue an inmate." All BOP staff members receive training on this policy while attending introductory training for all new employees, and yearly thereafter during annual refresher training. BOP investigators receive in-depth interviewing training while attending the Investigative Intelligence training. All correctional staff members also are trained to report any injuries of inmates to the Operations Lieutenant immediately for investigation.

99.   Within DHS, U.S. Customs and Border Protection (CBP) operates an Advanced Training Center that currently hosts two separate courses designed for front-line personnel who determine admissibility and/or the need for criminal prosecution. All attendees are instructed in the requirement to treat interviewees humanely and professionally, and this training is reinforced throughout the individual's career. CBP further ensures that all claims of abuse and/or mistreatment are documented and immediately forwarded to the appropriate investigating office.

100.   At the DHS/ICE Academy, the ICE Special Agent Training program provides basic information on humane methods of interrogating suspects in furtherance of an investigation as well as guidelines for criminal and administrative enforcement operations. At any time during an ICE investigation when an individual is identified as a possible victim of torture or cruel or inhumane treatment, agents are instructed to work with the Human Rights Violators and War Crimes Unit, ICE Homeland Security Investigations Headquarters, as well as the identified ICE Victim Assistance Specialists or Coordinators, who coordinate referrals for victim assistance services with the appropriate social service providers and non-governmental organizations. They also work with the relevant Victim-Witness Coordinators at DOJ or any other law enforcement based victim specialist connected with the investigation. Specific training concerning the prohibition on torture and cruel, inhuman, and degrading treatment for ICE's state and local

partners who participate in the detention model of the Immigration Authority Delegation Program (IADP or "287(g) program") is also provided at the ICE Academy. Interrogation rules, instructions, and methods are covered. Instruction on identifying signs of torture and cruel, inhuman and degrading treatment is covered in the victim assistance section. State and local law enforcement personnel participating in the detention model of the 287(g) program are instructed to report such incidents to ICE through their local chain of command and ICE-assigned supervisors.

Response to issues raised in Question 16(b).

101.   The United States recognizes the important role the Effective Investigation and Documentation of Torture and Other Cruel, Inhuman or Degrading Treatment or Punishment (Istanbul Protocol) can play in international efforts to promote the effective investigation and documentation of torture and other ill-treatment.[3] U.S. agencies involved with detainees are aware of the need to recognize and document such evidence as part of the effort to bring to justice those who violate the law. Medical personnel associated with such agencies who treat detainees are trained to detect signs of abuse or neglect and are required to report any such signs to appropriate supervising authorities if misconduct is suspected.

Response to issues raised in Question 16(c).

102.   In an on-going effort to lessen the likelihood of abusive treatment, the Army Inspector General conducts an in-depth biennial inspection of all aspects of detention operations. The inspection team includes intelligence professionals who look specifically at interrogation operations. In addition, all combatant commanders who have detention responsibilities conduct semi-annual detention operations assessments, which are also supported by intelligence professionals who carefully examine interrogation operations. Both the biennial and semi-annual assessments provide DoD with the ability to ascertain the effectiveness of its training protocols. Any lessons learned, noted shortfalls, or recommendations are provided to training institutions to ensure they receive appropriate feedback on the results of their training curriculum.

---

[3] The United States notes that the Istanbul Protocol was prepared as a collaborative effort by forensic scientists, physicians, psychologists, human-rights monitors and lawyers from a number of countries; although not legally binding, the Principles contained in Annex 1 were annexed to General Assembly resolution 55/89 of December 4, 2000 and Commission on Human Rights resolution 2000/43 of April 20, 2000, both adopted by consensus.

103.   The DHS/ICE Office of Professional Responsibility (OPR) investigates allegations of violations of laws and ICE policy, including allegations of torture or cruel, inhumane, or degrading treatment, which are then forwarded to the DHS/OIG. The OIG may retain the case for its own action, or, if the matter relates to an ICE employee or contractor, return the case to ICE/OPR or DOJ for action. The ICE Office of Detention Oversight inspects detention facilities to determine their compliance with detention standards that include ensuring safe and humane treatment of detainees.

104.   Any suspected misconduct in DOJ/BOP facilities must be reported to internal investigative staff and/or DOJ/OIG. BOP facilities are routinely audited to ensure compliance with detention standards that include ensuring safe and humane treatment of detainees.

17. Please indicate steps taken to ensure that acts of health personnel are in full conformity with principle No. 2 of the Principles of Medical Ethics relevant to the Role of Health Personnel in the Protection of Prisoners and Detainees against Torture and Other Cruel, Inhuman or Degrading Treatment or Punishment. In this respect, please provide information on the participation and role of health personnel in interrogations of terror suspects, including in secret detention facilities.

105.   U.S. practice is consistent with principle No. 2 of the non-binding Principles of Medical Ethics relevant to the Role of Health Personnel in the Protection of Prisoners and Detainees against Torture and Other Cruel, Inhuman or Degrading Treatment or Punishment. The prohibition on torture under U.S. law is absolute and, as provided in the Detainee Treatment Act of 2005, no individual in the custody or under the physical control of the U.S. government, regardless of nationality or physical location, shall be subject to cruel, inhuman, or degrading treatment or punishment. Provisions applicable to BOP medical staff are delineated in Program Statement 6010.02 Health Services Administration. The policy reaffirms the agency's position that all inmates have value as human beings, deserve medically necessary health care, and should be treated with a focus on compassionate care. Medical staff who deviate from the standards of care are addressed through administrative discipline, professional license referrals, and personal liability in the federal courts. All staff members are provided training concerning the use of force against inmates upon employment with the agency, and in refresher classes provided annually. Medical staff are part of this training, and also receive training on several areas concerning standards of care on a frequent basis. Medical staff are subject to the same provisions concerning

this matter as other BOP staff. Program Statement 3420.09, Standards of Employee Conduct, states, "An employee may not use brutality, physical violence, or intimidation towards inmates, or use of any force beyond that which is reasonably necessary to subdue an inmate." Program Statement 5566.06, Use of Force, authorizes staff to use force only as a last resort, and limits the amount of force used to only that which is necessary to gain control of an inmate, protect human safety, prevent serious property damage, and to ensure security and good order. The Bureau's policies concerning interrogation are available at www.bop.gov.

106. DoD Instruction 2310.08E (Medical Program Support for Detainee Operations) Section 1.3, issued on June 6, 2006, "[r]eaffirms the responsibility of health care personnel to protect and treat, in the context of a professional treatment relationship and established principles of medical practice, all detainees in the control of the Armed Forces during military operations. This includes enemy prisoners of war, retained personnel, civilian internees, and other detainees." Section 4.1 of the instruction goes on to establish basic principles for healthcare personnel, among which are included the duty to uphold humane treatment and ensure that no individual in U.S. custody is subject to cruel, inhuman, or degrading treatment or punishment (in accordance with U.S. law); and the "duty to protect detainees' physical and mental health and provide treatment for disease . . . guided by professional judgments and standards similar to those applied to personnel of the U.S. Armed Forces." Paragraph 4.1.3 states "Health care personnel shall not be involved in any professional provider-patient treatment relationship with detainees the purpose of which is not solely to evaluate, protect, or improve their physical and mental health." Paragraph 4.1.5 states "Health care personnel shall not certify, or participate in the certification of, the fitness of detainees for any form of treatment or punishment that is not in accordance with applicable law, or participate in any way in the administration of any such treatment or punishment." Paragraph 4.5 establishes reportable incident requirements related to observed or suspected violation of applicable standards for treatment of detainees. In addition, section 4.6 establishes a requirement that "health care personnel involved in the treatment of detainees or other detainee matters receive appropriate training on applicable policies and procedures regarding the care and treatment of detainees." With regard to the role of health personnel in interrogations, behavioral science consultants (BSCs) are the only medical personnel who may provide advice concerning interrogations of detainees and they may do so only when the interrogations are fully in accordance with applicable law and properly issued interrogation

instructions. BSCs are not involved in the medical treatment of detainees and do not access medical records.

Article 11

18. The Committee and the Human Rights Committee have expressed their concern that the State party authorized the use of enhanced interrogation techniques, such as methods involving sexual humiliation, "waterboarding", "short shackling" and using dogs to induce fear (para. 24 and CCPR/C/USA/CO/3/Rev.1, para. 13). In this respect, please describe steps taken to ensure that interrogation rules, instructions or methods do not derogate from the principle of absolute prohibition of torture. Furthermore, please:

(a) Provide updated information on the content of the Army Field Manual on Interrogation and its conformity with the Convention;
(b) Clarify if the standard for interrogation set in the manual is binding on all components of the State party, including intelligence agencies and private contractors who act on their behalf;
(c) Provide information with regard to the Central Intelligence Agency (CIA) interrogation manual;
(d) Indicate whether all interrogation techniques used in practice are in conformity with the Convention;
(e) Describe any steps taken to adopt legislation that explicitly prohibits interrogation techniques amounting to torture, such as those identified by the Committee in its previous concluding observations.

107.   As discussed in response to Questions 5 and 6, in E.O. 13491, Ensuring Lawful Interrogations, President Obama directed that individuals detained in any armed conflict shall in all circumstances be treated humanely, and shall not be subjected to any interrogation technique or approach, or any treatment related to interrogation, that is not authorized by and listed in the Army Field Manual, without prejudice to the use by federal law enforcement agencies of authorized, non-coercive techniques of interrogation that are designed to elicit voluntary statements and do not involve the use of force, threats, or promises. The manual explicitly prohibits threats, coercion, physical abuse, and "waterboarding." The executive order also revoked previous executive directives, orders, and regulations to the extent inconsistent with that order.

108.   Actions prohibited by the Army Field Manual with respect to intelligence interrogations include, but are not limited to: forcing the detainee to be naked, perform sexual acts, or pose in a sexual manner; placing hoods or sacks over the head of a detainee or using duct tape over the

41

eyes; applying beatings, electronic shock, burns, or other forms of physical pain; "waterboarding"; using military working dogs; inducing hypothermia or heat injury; conducting mock executions; and depriving the detainee of necessary food, water, or medical care. The Army Field Manual also provides guidance to be used while formulating interrogation plans for approval. It states: "In attempting to determine if a contemplated approach or technique should be considered prohibited . . . consider these two tests before submitting the plan for approval:

- If the proposed approach technique were used by the enemy against one of your fellow soldiers, would you believe the soldier had been abused?
- Could your conduct in carrying out the proposed technique violate a law or regulation? Keep in mind that even if you personally would not consider your actions to constitute abuse, the law may be more restrictive.

If you answer yes to either of these tests, the contemplated action should not be conducted."

Response to issues raised in Question 18(a).

109.   The Army Field Manual was promulgated on September 6, 2006 and supersedes all previous versions of the manual. It lists the 18 Congressionally-approved interrogation approaches and the one Congressionally-approved interrogation technique (separation) that may be used with detainees, including the restrictions and limitations on their use discussed above.

110.   Interrogations undertaken in compliance with the Army Field Manual are consistent with U.S. domestic and international law obligations. For example, the Army Field Manual states that "[a]ll captured or detained personnel, regardless of status, shall be treated humanely, and in accordance with the Detainee Treatment Act of 2005 and DoD Directive 2310.1E . . . and no person in the custody or under the control of DoD, regardless of nationality or physical location, shall be subject to torture or cruel, inhuman, or degrading treatment or punishment, in accordance with and as defined in U.S. law." The Army Field Manual is available at www.fas.org/irp/doddir/army/fm2-22-3.pdf.

Response to issues raised in Question 18(b).

111.   The United States confirms that the interrogation approaches and techniques in the Army Field Manual are binding on the U.S. military, as well as all federal government agencies,

including the intelligence agencies, with respect to individuals in U.S. custody or under U.S. effective control in any armed conflict, without prejudice to authorized non-coercive techniques of federal law enforcement agencies. This requirement was established in E.O. 13491, and the Special Task Force created by that E.O. specifically affirmed that the Army Field Manual provides appropriate guidance on interrogation for military interrogators and determined that no additional or different guidance was necessary for other agencies. The Special Task Force explained that its conclusions rested on its unanimous assessment, including that of the Intelligence Community, that the practices and techniques identified by the Army Field Manual or currently used by law enforcement provide adequate and effective means of conducting interrogations.

112.   With respect to private contractors, § 1038 of the 2010 National Defense Authorization Act (Public Law 111-84) banned contractor personnel from interrogating any individual "under the effective control of DoD or otherwise under detention in a DoD facility in connection with hostilities" unless the Secretary of Defense determines that a waiver to this prohibition is vital to the national security interests of the United States and waives the prohibition for a period of up to 60 days or renews the waiver for one additional 30-day period. The Department does not currently employ contract interrogators. This does not prohibit contractors from performing tasks ancillary to interrogations. DoD policy (DoD Directive 3115.09) applies the humane treatment standard to contractors performing these ancillary tasks and specifies that their contracts must "comply with the same rules, procedures, policies, and laws pertaining to detainee operations and interrogations as apply to Government personnel in such positions."

Response to issues raised in Question 18(c).
113.   Consistent with E.O. No. 13491, the CIA does not use any interrogation measures not permitted by the Army Field Manual.

Response to issues raised in Question 18(d).
114.   As discussed above, all interrogation approaches and techniques permitted by the Army Field Manual as well as authorized, non-coercive techniques of interrogation for federal law enforcement agencies, are in conformity with the Convention.

Response to issues raised in Question 18(e).

115.   As demonstrated throughout this report and in particular the responses to Questions 1 and 7, the prohibition on torture under U.S. law is absolute. No further legislation prohibiting specific actions constituting torture or cruel, inhuman, or degrading treatment or punishment is required in order to comply with U.S. obligations under the CAT.

116.   In addition to generally applicable legislation, DTA § 1002 specifically provides that "[n]o person in the custody or under the effective control of DoD or under detention in a DoD facility shall be subject to any treatment or technique of interrogation not authorized by and listed in the U.S. Army Field Manual on Intelligence Interrogation." Furthermore, DTA § 1003 provides that "no individual in the custody or under the physical control of the U.S. government, regardless of nationality or physical location, shall be subject to cruel, inhuman, or degrading treatment or punishment." This prohibition is without geographical limitation.

19. Please provide updated information on the composition and functioning of the inter-agency task force established by an executive order to evaluate the interrogation practices allowed by the Army Field Manual. Please also elaborate on the work of the agency, in particular on whether it has recommended any changes.

117.   E.O. 13491 provided that the Special Task Force be chaired by the Attorney General or his designee and that the Director of National Intelligence and the Secretary of Defense, or their designees, serve as Co-Vice-Chairs; other members of the Special Task Force included representatives of the Secretaries of State and Homeland Security, the Director of the CIA, the Chairman of the Joint Chiefs of Staff, and other representatives as determined by the Chair.

118.   As indicated in response to Question 18(b), in August 2009 the Special Task Force concluded that the Army Field Manual provides appropriate guidance on interrogation for military interrogators, and that no additional or different guidance was necessary for other agencies. The Special Task Force concluded, moreover, that the United States could improve its ability to interrogate the most dangerous terrorists by forming a specialized interrogation group, or High Value Detainee Interrogation Group, which is discussed in response to Question 21.

20. Please indicate if the International Committee of the Red Cross is granted access to all places of detention in any territory under its jurisdiction, including Bagram Airbase in Afghanistan and Diego Garcia, and under which conditions.

119.   The United States notes paragraph 6 of this report. Executive Order 13491 requires that "[a]ll departments and agencies of the Federal Government shall provide the International Committee of the Red Cross with notification of, and timely access to, any individual detained in any armed conflict in the custody or under the effective control of an officer, employee, or other agent of the United States Government or detained within a facility owned, operated, or controlled by a department or agency of the U.S. Government, consistent with Department of Defense regulations and policies." (Section 4(b)). Additional information on detainee registration and ICRC access is provided in response to Question 4(a).

120.   The relationship the United States maintains with the ICRC is a productive one, based on confidentiality. The U.S. government maintains an ongoing dialogue with ICRC representatives, and addresses any concerns they may raise at appropriate levels of command and civilian leadership.

121.   As stated in response to Question 5(a), the United States does not operate and has not operated a detention facility on Diego Garcia.

21. Please provide updated information on the establishment, composition and functioning of the "High-Value Interrogation Group", responsible for the interrogation of high-value detainees. Please provide detailed information on steps taken to ensure that the unit will only use interrogation techniques that are in conformity with the Convention. Furthermore, information should be provided on the authority responsible for monitoring such unit.

122.   The High-Value Detainee Interrogation Group (HIG) was established as recommended by the Special Task Force, which concluded that the HIG could improve the U.S. ability to interrogate the most dangerous terrorists by bringing together the most effective and experienced interrogators and support personnel from the FBI, the CIA, and DoD to conduct interrogations in a manner that will continue to strengthen national security consistent with the rule of law. The Special Task Force recommended that this specialized interrogation group develop a set of best practices and disseminate them for training purposes to agencies that conduct interrogations. In addition, the Special Task Force recommended that a scientific research program for

interrogation be established to study the comparative effectiveness of interrogation approaches and techniques, with the goal of identifying the existing techniques that are most effective and developing new lawful techniques to improve intelligence interrogations.

123.   The HIG is an interagency body that is administratively housed within the FBI. The HIG has a Director, who is an FBI employee, and two Deputy Directors, who are drawn from the CIA and DoD. The HIG's Mobile Interrogation Teams bring together experienced interrogators, analysts, subject matter experts, behavioral science experts, linguists, and others drawn from across the intelligence community, military and law enforcement to conduct and/or provide support to interrogation of high-value detainees.

124.   Interrogations conducted or supported by the HIG are consistent with the provisions of E.O. 13491 and with U.S. domestic and international law, including the CAT.

125.   Under its charter of operations, the HIG complies with the humane treatment requirements set forth in E.O. 13491, as well as all other U.S. law, policies and guidance regarding the treatment and interrogation of detainees. HIG personnel also have a duty to comply with their home agencies' operations, and report legal issues regarding compliance with the law to the proper authority. DOJ in its role as HIG legal counsel, in coordination with attorneys at participating agencies and the National Security Council and the White House, is responsible for evaluating legal issues concerning HIG compliance with US domestic and international legal obligations regarding the treatment and interrogation of detainees and other appropriate matters.

Articles 12 and 13

22. Please indicate if the State party has investigated, prosecuted and punished perpetrators under the federal extraterritorial criminal torture statute, as recommended by the Committee in its previous concluding observations (para. 13). If so, please provide further information on the relevant cases.

126.   The United States has investigated and prosecuted allegations of extraterritorial torture over which it has jurisdiction. On October 30, 2008, Roy M. Belfast, Jr., son of Charles G. Taylor, former president of Liberia, was convicted of crimes related to torture in Liberia between April 1999 and July 2003 under the U.S. extraterritorial torture statute, 18 U.S.C. 2340A. On January 9, 2009, he was sentenced to 97 years in prison. The prosecution of these torture claims

was the first under the Torture Convention Implementation Act, 18 U.S.C. 2340A et seq. Further information on the Belfast case is provided in 2011 ICCPR Report ¶ 181, incorporated herein by reference.

23. In light of the Committee's previous concluding observations, please provide information on:

(a) Steps taken to ensure that all forms of torture and ill-treatment of detainees by its military or civilian personnel, in any territory under its de facto and de jure jurisdiction, as well as in any other place under its effective control, is promptly, impartially and thoroughly investigated, and that all those responsible, including senior military and civilian officials authorizing, acquiescing or consenting in any way to such acts committed by their subordinates are prosecuted and appropriately punished, in accordance with the seriousness of the crime (para. 26). Are all suspects in prima facie cases of torture and ill-treatment as a rule suspended or reassigned during the process of investigation?

(b) The mandate of the prosecutor in charge of the preliminary review into whether United States laws were violated by CIA officers and contractors during the interrogation of detainees at places outside the United States, including Guantánamo Bay. Please elaborate on the outcome of this investigation and, if applicable, on the steps taken to hold the responsible persons accountable.

Response to issues raised in Question 23(a).

127.   The United States notes paragraph 6 of this Report. U.S. law provides jurisdiction in a number of ways that could be relied on for criminal prosecution of torture and ill-treatment of detainees, including the following:

- Filing criminal charges, which can lead to investigation and possible prosecution. Under 18 U.S.C. 242, DOJ can prosecute any person who, under color of law, subjects a victim in any state, territory, commonwealth, possession, or district to the deprivation of any rights or privileges secured or protected by the Constitution or laws of the United States. The government may also bring criminal prosecution for use of force or threat of force to violate a person's right under the 1964 Civil Rights Act, 18 U.S.C. 245. Abuse of police power, denial of rights guaranteed by the Constitution and denials of due process can be reached under these statutes. Under 18 U.S.C. 2340 and 2340A, DOJ can prosecute U.S. military and civilian personnel who, outside the United States, commit or attempt to commit the crime of torture, which is defined as an act committed by a person acting under color of law specifically intended to inflict severe physical or mental pain or

47

suffering upon another person within his custody or physical control if the alleged offender is present in the United States or is a national of the United States;

- Challenging official action or inaction through judicial procedures in state courts and under state law, based on statutory or constitutional provisions. Any court, from the lowest court to the U.S. Supreme Court, may consider such constitutional claims, although normally they must be raised at the earliest opportunity.

128.   In addition to the remedies discussed above, federal, state and local officials as well as private persons who violate the rights of others may be subject to prosecution under a host of generic federal and state criminal statutes. DoD personnel may be subject to criminal prosecution under the Uniform Code of Military Justice, 10 U.S.C. 801-940.

129.   The U.S. Armed Forces conduct prompt and independent investigations into all credible allegations concerning mistreatment of detainees. Detention facilities are inspected on a regular basis to ensure compliance with DoD regulations and to determine if improvements in operations are necessary. In addition, the U.S. Armed Forces have several independent criminal investigative agencies, whose function is to investigate allegations of criminal behavior. The U.S. Government has attempted to address all credible allegations as quickly and as fully as possible. To that end, more than 100 service members have been court martialed for mistreatment of detainees with an 86% conviction rate. Others have faced administrative sanctions, including separation from the service.

130.   This issue is addressed further in the 2011 ICCPR Report ¶¶ 536-546 incorporated herein by reference. Examples of specific prosecutions are provided in response to Questions 24 and 51.

131.   In March 2010, DOJ announced the merger of two Criminal Division components that were responsible for investigating and prosecuting various types of human rights violations. The creation of the new component, the Human Rights and Special Prosecutions Section (HRSP), underscores the commitment of United States authorities to end impunity for torturers and other human rights violators. HRSP and other DOJ components have prosecuted U.S. military and civilian personnel who have perpetrated human rights violations outside the United States. By combining the resources, skills, and expertise of two experienced and accomplished law

enforcement teams working on these cases, the merger was intended to enhance the government's effectiveness in pursuing violators and denying them safe haven in the United States. In investigating these cases, HRSP works closely with U.S. Attorneys' Offices, DHS/ICE, the FBI, and other authorities as appropriate. Both ICE and the FBI operate specialized units devoted to investigating human rights violation suspects.

132. The DHS Office for Civil Rights and Civil Liberties (CRCL) investigates complaints from the public alleging violations of civil rights or civil liberties by DHS personnel, programs, or activities. In fiscal year (FY) 2012, for example, CRCL opened 59 complaints alleging poor or inhumane conditions of detention, and 13 complaints alleging abuses of authority by DHS employees or contractors. Some of these were referred to DHS component agencies, primarily ICE and CBP, for investigation; most were retained for investigation and further action by CRCL.

133. USG employees investigated for abusing or mistreating detainees are prohibited from further contact with detainees until the investigation is concluded. If an investigation determines that an employee has engaged in this inappropriate conduct, the employee may be subject to criminal prosecution or disciplinary action, which may include termination of employment.

134. The United States continues to explore ways to enhance its investigative and prosecutorial capabilities in these cases, including through enactment of additional legislation when appropriate, to combat impunity and promote deterrence.

Response to issues raised in Question 23(b).
135. In August 2009, the Attorney General announced that he had ordered "a preliminary review into whether federal laws were violated in connection with interrogation of specific detainees at overseas locations." See www.justice.gov/ag/speeches/2009/ag-speech-0908241.html. Assistant U.S. Attorney John Durham assembled an investigative team of experienced professionals to recommend to the Attorney General whether a full investigation was warranted "into whether the law was violated in connection with the interrogation of certain detainees." Following a two year investigation, on June 30, 2011, the Justice Department announced that it was opening a full criminal investigation into the deaths of two individuals in CIA custody overseas, and that it had concluded that further investigation into the other cases

examined in the preliminary investigation was not warranted. See
www.justice.gov/opa/pr/2011/June/11-ag-861.html. These investigations were closed in 2012
after DOJ determined that the admissible evidence would not be sufficient to obtain and sustain a
conviction beyond a reasonable doubt.

**24. Please describe steps taken to ensure prompt and effective investigation into any
allegations of torture or ill-treatment by private military and security companies and
prosecute alleged perpetrators. In this respect, please indicate if the Department of Justice
has strengthened its investigative resource capacity and appointed an independent
prosecutor, as recommended by the Working Group on mercenaries.**

136.   DoD Directive 3115.09 (DoD Intelligence Interrogations, Detainee Debriefings, and
Tactical Questioning) ¶ 4.c. states that "[o]nly DoD interrogators who are trained and certified in
accordance with the standards . . . may conduct DoD intelligence interrogations. DoD
intelligence interrogations shall be conducted only by personnel properly trained and certified to
DoD standards" Congress has now effectively barred civilian contractors from performing
interrogation functions, and has required private translators involved in interrogation operations
to undergo substantial training and to be subject to substantial oversight. See Ronald W. Reagan
National Defense Authorization Act for Fiscal Year 2010, Pub. L. No. 111-84, 1038, 123 Stat.
2451-2452 (2009); 75 Fed. Reg. 67,632-67,634 (2010). Section 1038 of the Act prohibits
contractor personnel from interrogating enemy prisoners of war, civilian internees, retained
personnel, other detainees, or any other individual who is in the custody or under the effective
control of DoD or otherwise under detention in a DoD facility in connection with hostilities,
unless the Secretary of Defense determines that a waiver to this prohibition is vital to the national
security interests of the United States and waives the prohibition for a period of up to 60 days or
renews the waiver for one additional 30-day period. The Department does not currently employ
contract interrogators.

137.   Several cases have been brought against contractors under the Military Extraterritorial
Jurisdiction Act and the Special Maritime and Territorial Jurisdiction (SMTJ). Convictions of
David Passaro and Don Ayala under these authorities are discussed in 2011 ICCPR ¶¶ 533 and
534, incorporated herein by reference. The availability of criminal and civil remedies for all
forms of torture and ill-treatment is discussed in response to Questions 23(a) and 27(a).

138.   In addition, domestic legislative efforts continue to pass a Civilian Extraterritorial Jurisdiction Act (CEJA) that provides clear and unambiguous jurisdiction to prosecute non-DoD personnel for overseas misconduct. CEJA's enactment has been supported by the Executive Branch. It was not passed by the 112th Congress, however, and has not been reintroduced in the current Congress to date.

139.   At the international level, the U.S. government actively engaged in the development of the Montreux Document on pertinent international legal obligations and good practices for States related to operations of private military and security companies during armed conflict, and the International Code of Conduct for Private Security Service Providers (Code). The latter initiative has the potential to improve private security contractor (PSC) compliance with applicable laws and respect for human rights, and to provide additional tools for identifying, avoiding, and remediating impacts that PSCs may have on communities and other stakeholders. DOS, along with other federal agencies including DoD, is actively engaged in ongoing efforts to establish a credible governance and oversight mechanism for the Code.

140.   DOJ has significantly strengthened its capabilities, particularly by creating the Criminal Division's HRSP discussed in response to Question 23(a). Moreover, the FBI has expanded its efforts in the area of human rights enforcement. The appointment of John Durham as Special Prosecutor is discussed in response to Question 23(b).

25. As requested by the Committee in its previous concluding observations, please provide updated information on the investigations and prosecution relating to the allegations of torture perpetrated in areas 2 and 3 of the Chicago Police Department (para. 25). In this respect, please provide detailed information on the charges filed against Jon Burge and, if applicable, on the outcome of this case. Furthermore, please indicate if any other police officers have been brought to justice in this case.

141.   On June 28, 2010, a federal jury in Chicago convicted former Chicago Police Department (CPD) Commander Jon Burge on perjury and obstruction charges related to his denials that he participated in the torture of suspects in police custody in the 1980s. The jury found that Burge lied and obstructed justice in November 2003 when he provided false statements in a civil lawsuit that alleged that he and others tortured and abused people in their custody. On January 21, 2011, Burge was sentenced to 54 months in prison. His conviction was upheld on appeal on April 2, 2013. United States v. Burge, 711 F.3d 803 (7th Cir. 2013). Mr. Burge had been

suspended by the Chicago Police Department in 1991 and fired in 1993 over allegations of abuse.

142.   During the trial, several victims testified that they had been tortured by Burge and other officers who worked for him in area two of the CPD. Various witnesses testified that the officers administered electric shocks to their genitals, suffocated them with typewriter covers, threatened them with loaded guns, and burned them on radiators. The jury found that Burge had lied under oath when he claimed that he did not participate in any of these acts of torture, and that he was unaware of any other officers having done so. Investigations into allegations of abuse by other CPD officers, and related false statements by those officers, are ongoing.

26. Please provide detailed information on the procedures in place to review the circumstances of detention, as well as on steps taken to ensure that the status of detainees is available to all detainees. In this respect, please elaborate on the status and content of the Military Commission Act, as well as its conformity with the Convention.

143.   The United States notes that in ¶ 27 of its 2006 Concluding Observations, the Committee indicated that its concern with review of circumstances of detention and ensuring that status of detainees is available to all detainees arises in particular in the context of military detention at Guantanamo and in Iraq and Afghanistan.

144.   As noted in response to Question 8(c), the U.S. Supreme Court has determined that habeas corpus jurisdiction extends to noncitizens detained by DoD at Guantanamo (Rasul v. Bush, 542 U.S. 466 (2004), and Boumediene v. Bush, 553 U.S. 723 (2008)) and to U.S. citizens detained in effective U.S. custody in Iraq (Munaf v. Geren, 553 U.S. 674 (2008)).

145.   As also discussed in response to Question 8(c), President Obama issued E.O. 13567 on March 7, 2011, establishing a new robust periodic review process for Guantanamo detainees that includes the ability to present information, call certain witnesses, and receive the assistance of counsel. In 2009 review procedures were also improved for detainees held at the theater internment facility at Bagram airfield in Afghanistan. Safeguards to ensure humane treatment of detainees who were previously held by the United States in Iraq and have been transferred to Iraqi custody are discussed in response to Question 12. As noted there, the last detainee held in

U.S. physical custody in Iraq was transferred to Iraqi custody prior to the expiration of the U.S.-Iraq security agreement on December 31, 2011.

146.   The United States believes that the Military Commissions Act of 2009 is fully consistent with the Convention. The terms of the Act are described in response to Question 8(b).

Article 14

27. Pursuant the Committee's previous concluding observations (para. 28), please provide:

    (a) Information on steps taken to ensure that mechanisms to obtain full redress, compensation and rehabilitation are accessible to all victims of acts or torture, including sexual violence, perpetrated by its officials. In this respect, please provide information about any reparation programmes, including psychological treatment and other forms of rehabilitation, provided to victims of torture and ill-treatment, as well as about the allocation of adequate resources to ensure the effective functioning of such programmes.
    (b) Statistical data, disaggregated by sex and age, on the number of requests for redress made, the number granted and the amounts ordered and those actually provided in each case. In particular, information should be provided on the number of cases filed by detainees, including under the Foreign Claims Act, since the examination of the last periodic report in 2006.

Response to issues raised in Question 27(a).
147.   U.S. law provides various avenues for seeking redress in cases of torture and other violations of constitutional and statutory rights relevant to the Convention. A wide range of civil remedies includes injunctions, compensatory and/or punitive damages and equitable relief. In addition, where Congress has so provided, the federal government may bring civil actions to enjoin acts or patterns of conduct that violate constitutional rights, including those that would amount to acts of torture. Finally, as discussed in response to Questions 1, 22 and 23(a), U.S. law provides for criminal prosecution of individuals believed to have committed such crimes. A detailed list of available criminal and civil actions is provided in the CCD ¶ 158, incorporated herein by reference. Included in the list, as to torture specifically, the Torture Victim Protection Act, enacted in 1992 (28 U.S.C. 1350 note) created a cause of action in federal courts against "[a]n individual . . . [a]cting under actual or apparent authority, or color of law, of any foreign nation" available to individuals regardless of nationality, including U.S. nationals, who are victims of official torture or extrajudicial killing. As discussed in the 2006 Response to List of

Issues at 78-79, claims for alleged detainee abuse or maltreatment made against DoD are resolved through the Military Departments.

Response to issues raised in Question 27(b).

148.   Illustrative cases demonstrating the ability of victims of sexual violence to obtain redress in the United States are set forth in response to Question 32(d).

28. Please indicate if the State party has amended the Prison Litigation Reform Act, including to guarantee the right of victims to bring civil actions, as recommended by the Committee in its previous concluding observations (para. 29).

Response to issues raised in Question 28.

149.   In ¶ 29 of its Concluding Observations, the Committee stated its concern with "section 1997e(e) of the 1995 Prison Litigation Reform Act which provides that no federal civil action may be brought by a prisoner for mental or emotional injury suffered while in custody without a prior showing of physical injury."

150.   This provision does not preclude redress through civil actions for such mental or emotional injury. There is ample decisional authority from multiple federal courts interpreting the language of 42 U.S.C. 1997e(e) to permit incarcerated persons to seek redress other than compensatory damages for substandard conditions of confinement. Most importantly, inmates can seek injunctions ordering prison managers to correct conditions that are constitutionally infirm. See, e.g., Mitchell v. Horn, 318 F.3d 523, 533-34 (3rd Cir. 2003) ("§ 1997e(e) does not apply to claims seeking injunctive or declaratory relief").

151.   Inmates may also bring constitutional tort claims against prison managers responsible for unconstitutional conditions of confinement. "Section 1997e(e)'s requirement that a prisoner demonstrate physical injury before he or she can recover for mental or emotional injury applies only to claims for compensatory damages. Claims seeking nominal or punitive damages are typically not 'for' mental or emotional injury but rather 'to vindicate constitutional rights' or 'to deter or punish egregious violations of constitutional rights,' respectively." Id. at 533. Although the decisions vary in respect of the quantum of damages recoverable, compare Calhoun v. DeTella, 319 F.3d 936, 941 (7th Cir. 2003) (permitting inmates to seek both punitive and nominal damages) with Hutchins v. McDaniels, 512 F.3d 193, 196-98 (5th Cir. 2007) (inmate

may seek nominal damages), there is no question that inmates may bring a civil action and receive a judicial ruling on the challenge.

152.   In light of the availability of these avenues of recovery, the United States has not amended section 1997e(e).

Article 15

29. In light of the Committee's previous concluding observations, please provide information on steps taken by the State party to ensure that its obligations under articles 13 and 15 are fulfilled in all circumstances, including in the context of the military commissions (para. 30). Please inform the Committee whether the State party has established an independent mechanism to guarantee the rights of all detainees in custody.

153.   As discussed in response to Question 3, under U.S. law, every U.S. official, wherever he or she may be, is prohibited from engaging in torture or in cruel, inhuman or degrading treatment or punishment, at all times, and in all places. For information concerning the right to complain under Article 13 more generally, see response to Questions 28 and 42(a).

154.   As to the exclusion from evidence of statements established to have been made as a result of torture under Article 15, the U.S. Supreme Court has long held that persons protected under the Fifth Amendment to the U.S. Constitution, which commands that no person "shall be compelled in any criminal trial to be a witness against himself" will be protected from the use of their involuntary statements (or evidence derived from such statements) in any subsequent criminal trial in courts of the United States. See Bram v. United States, 168 U .S. 532 (1897). This protection extends to criminal trials in state courts, Malloy v. Hogan, 378 U.S. 1 (1964), and under the Indian Civil Rights Act of 1968, 25 U.S.C. 1302 ("no Indian tribe in exercising powers of self-government shall . . . compel any person in any criminal case to be a witness against himself").

155.   Specifically regarding detainees at Guantanamo, the ICRC visits regularly and serves as an independent mechanism through which detainees can raise complaints. In addition, the detainees can and do raise complaints directly with the U.S. military at Guantanamo, which maintains robust internal review procedures. If a credible allegation of torture were raised by a

defendant in a military commission proceeding, DoD would conduct an investigation in accordance with relevant DoD policy. See responses to Questions 16(a) and 23(a).

156.   In the context of military commissions, the Military Commissions Act of 2009 prohibits admission of any statement obtained by the use of torture or by cruel, inhuman, or degrading treatment, as defined by the Detainee Treatment Act of 2005, in a military commission proceeding, except against a person accused of torture or such treatment as evidence that the statement was made. 10 U.S.C. 948r. No other exception to this prohibition on admissibility of such statements is permitted in the rules governing admission of hearsay evidence or otherwise. This prohibition is also incorporated into Rule 304(a)(1) of the Rules for Military Commissions. For any statement made by an accused that was not obtained by torture or cruel, inhuman, and degrading treatment, the MCA 2009 sets up a rigorous standard for determining admissibility that considers the voluntariness and reliability of the statement and whether the conduct of those taking the statement was lawful.

157.   In the military commission proceedings in Hamdan, the Military Judge excluded statements made by Hamdan at Panshir and Bagram bases because of "the conditions under which they were made." In another case, during the pre-trial phase, counsel for Mohammed Jawad made several allegations that their client was mistreated by both Afghan and U.S. personnel. In response to these allegations, the judge found that Mr. Jawad was mistreated by Afghan personnel and ordered the suppression of all of Mr. Jawad's confessions of guilt, including subsequent confessions made to U.S. personnel.

Article 16

30. With reference to the Committee's previous concluding observations, please provide information on measures taken to prohibit and prevent enforced disappearances in any territory under its jurisdiction, and prosecute and punish perpetrators (para. 18).

158.   U.S. federal and state criminal laws proscribe unlawful acts that can constitute enforced disappearance. For example, the federal kidnapping statute criminalizes kidnapping persons across state or international lines, in the SMTJ or in the special aircraft jurisdiction of the United States and provides for imprisonment up to life and, if the death of any person results, capital

punishment or life imprisonment. 18 U.S.C. 1201. Similar statutes exist in states of the United States for kidnapping that occurs solely within the state.

159.   As discussed in response to Question 5(a), the United States does not operate any secret places of detention. The ICRC is provided regular status updates on all individuals detained by the United States in connection with armed conflict, consistent with DoD policy, and is notified of detainee transfers out of U.S. custody. See response to Question 4 concerning requirements for public recordkeeping on all persons in custody.

160.   Throughout its responses in this report, the United States has provided extensive information on regulation of humane treatment of detainees, requirements for registration of detainees, and U.S. protections against transfer to torture.

31. Please address the following:

(a) Is the State party considering abolishing the death penalty?
(b) In light of the Committee's previous concluding observations, please provide information on steps taken to address the continuous concern that executions by lethal injection can cause severe pain and suffering (para. 31). In this respect, please elaborate on the events of the failed execution in the state of Ohio on 15 September 2009 and the proceedings following this, as well as on the fact that the revised execution procedure used by the state of California for carrying out executions continues to be lethal injection.
(c) Furthermore, please also provide information on the Nebraska Supreme Court's ruling that the use of the electric chair constitutes cruel and unusual punishment. Please indicate in how many states executions by electric chair are still performed.

Response to issues raised in Question 31(a).
161.   As elaborated below, six states in the United States have abolished capital punishment since the last report. At the federal level, the United States is not currently considering abolishing the death penalty, which is reserved for only the most serious crimes. However, Supreme Court cases have narrowed the categories of defendants against whom the death penalty may be applied at both the federal and state level, eliminating its availability for rape of a minor where the crime did not result, and was not intended to result, in the minor's death, Kennedy v. Louisiana, 554 U.S. 407 (2008); and for defendants who were under eighteen at the time of the crime, Roper v. Simmons, 543 U.S. 551 (2005), or have a severe intellectual disability ("mentally retarded"), Atkins v. Virginia, 536 U.S. 304 (2002). In addition, heightened procedural protections and guarantees apply in the context of capital punishment, which are well respected and enforced by

the courts. These issues are discussed further in the CCD ¶ 102 and the 2011 ICCPR Report ¶¶ 651-658, incorporated herein by reference.

162.   The number of states that have the death penalty, the number of inmates executed, and the size of the population on death row have all declined in the last decade, as discussed in the 2011 ICCPR Report ¶ 154, incorporated herein by reference. In recent years, the death penalty has been abolished in New York, New Jersey, New Mexico, Illinois, Connecticut, and most recently in Maryland on April 30, 2013. As of May 1, 2013, 32 states had laws permitting imposition of the death penalty – down from 38 states in 2000. On November 22, 2011, the Governor of Oregon declared a moratorium on its use in that state. In a number of other states, although capital punishment remains on the books, it is rarely, if ever, imposed. Six states that retain the death penalty, for example, have not conducted an execution in the last decade.

Response to issues raised in Question 31(b).
163.   The execution procedures utilized in the United States are carried out in a humane manner by appropriately trained and qualified personnel, and have been effectively utilized by the states and federal government. Lethal injection is the primary execution method used by all states that have the death penalty, as well as the federal government and military.

164.   In 2006 the Supreme Court decided that death row inmates may, under civil rights laws, challenge the manner in which death by lethal injection is carried out, Hill v. McDonough, 547 U.S. 573 (2006). Subsequently, in Baze v. Rees, 553 U.S. 35 (2008), a plurality of the Supreme Court reiterated that a method of execution does not violate the Eighth Amendment's prohibition against cruel and unusual punishment unless it creates an "objectively intolerable" risk that severe pain will be inflicted on the condemned inmate, and the state need not adopt an alternative method of execution unless it would significantly reduce a substantial risk of serious harm. Although the Court was divided as to the proper test for determining the constitutionality of a method of execution, a majority held that the state of Kentucky's three-drug lethal injection protocol – which mirrored the protocols followed by most states and the federal government at the time Baze was decided – did not constitute cruel and unusual punishment. Legal challenges continue in the lower courts in the wake of Baze, although the lower courts have generally rejected challenges to lethal injection protocols, including challenges to recently-adopted protocols that rely upon new drug combinations or on a single drug.

165.   Each state legislature has the ability to establish its own criminal punishments, so long as they are consistent with the limits placed by the U.S. and state Constitutions. In response to the failed execution of Romell Broom on September 15, 2009, the state of Ohio instituted an amended execution protocol in November 2009; courts in Ohio have rejected several legal challenges to the state's revised protocol.

166.   In December 2006, a U.S. District Court judge found that California's lethal injection protocol, as administered, violated the Eighth Amendment's prohibition of cruel and unusual punishment. Morales v. Tilton, 465 F. Supp. 2d 972 (N.D. Cal. 2006). Specifically, the court identified five deficiencies in California's protocol. In response, California's governor instructed the California Department of Corrections and Rehabilitation (CDCR) to conduct a thorough review of its protocol. The CDCR filed an amended protocol with the court in May 2007. Final regulations for lethal injections in California went into effect in August 2010.

167.   In June 2012 the Supreme Court of Arkansas ruled in Hobbs v. Jones that the state's lethal-injection statute violated the state constitution's separation-of-powers provision by delegating unfettered discretion to the state department of corrections to administer the death penalty. In August 2012 the U.S. Court of Appeals for the Fifth Circuit agreed to hear a challenge to Mississippi's lethal-injection protocol. Executions in Mississippi are now on hold. In September 2012 a Montana court ruled that the state's execution procedure was unconstitutional.

Response to issues raised in Question 31(c).
168.   In February 2008 the Nebraska Supreme Court held that use of the electric chair constitutes cruel and unusual punishment in violation of the Nebraska Constitution. State v. Mata, 745 N.W.2d 229 (Neb. 2008). This ruling by the Nebraska Supreme Court applies only to the state of Nebraska. In May 2009, the Nebraska legislature responded to the court decision by adopting lethal injection as the sole method of execution. No state uses the electric chair as a primary method of execution although execution by electrocution is an authorized method in eight states. Four of these eight states allow inmates to choose between lethal injection and electrocution; three of the eight states authorize inmates who committed offenses prior to a specific date to choose between lethal injection and electrocution; and one state authorizes electrocution as a method of execution if lethal injection is ever held unconstitutional.

32. With reference to the Committee's previous concluding observations (paras. 32 and 42), please provide:

(a) Information on steps taken to design and implement appropriate measures to prevent all sexual violence in all its detention centres. In this respect, please elaborate on the measures taken to implement the Prison Rape Elimination Act and on the standards developed by the National Prison Rape Elimination Commission in 2009 to detect, prevent, reduce, and punish prison rape, as well as on the implementation thereof.

(b) Please provide data on the prevalence of this problem.

(c) Please indicate steps taken to ensure that all allegations of violence in detention centres are investigated promptly and independently, as well as that perpetrators are prosecuted and appropriately sentenced.

(d) Information on steps taken to ensure that victims can seek redress, including appropriate compensation. Information should also be provided on the number of requests for redress made, the number granted and the amounts ordered and those actually provided in each case.

Please provide information on the impact and effectiveness of these measures in reducing cases of sexual violence in detention centres.

Response to issues raised in Question 32(a).

169.   The United States is taking extensive action at all levels of government to prevent sexual violence and other sexual victimization in its detention centers.

170.   The United States is actively working to address recommendations of the bipartisan National Prison Rape Elimination Commission (NPREC) established by the 2003 Prison Rape Elimination Act, Publ. L. No. 108-79 (PREA) as discussed in the 2011 ICCPR Report ¶¶ 226-230, incorporated herein by reference. DOJ regulations promulgated under PREA were issued as a final rule on May 17, 2012, effective August 20, 2012. See 28 C.F.R. Part 115. The regulations apply to the federal Bureau of Prisons and all DOJ components. States also must certify that all facilities in the state under the operational control of the state's executive branch are in compliance with the regulations, including facilities operated by private entities on behalf of the state's executive branch. Taking into account the public comments to its Proposed Rule, DOJ strengthened many of the regulations in the final rule, including greater protections for juvenile offenders in adult facilities; new restrictions on cross-gender viewing and searches; setting minimum staffing ratios in juvenile facilities; expanding medical and mental health care, including reproductive health care, for victims of prison rape; greater protections for lesbian, gay, bisexual, transgender, intersex, and gender non-conforming inmates; eliminating the deadline for submitting a grievance related to sexual abuse; and requiring independent audits of

all covered facilities. The regulations were immediately binding on BOP; state and local facilities were to begin implementation of the final standards as of August 20, 2012. The final rule is available at www.ojp.usdoj.gov/programs/pdfs/prea_final_rule.pdf.

171.   On May 17, 2012, the same day that DOJ issued its final rule under PREA, President Obama issued a Presidential Memorandum announcing that his Administration had concluded that "PREA applies to all Federal confinement facilities, including those operated by executive departments and agencies other than DOJ whether administered by the Federal Government or by a private organization on behalf of the Federal Government." The President also directed all agencies with federal confinement facilities not already subject to the DOJ final rule to issue rules or procedures necessary to satisfy the requirements of PREA. The Memorandum is available at www.whitehouse.gov/the-press-office/2012/05/17/presidential-memorandum-implementing-prison-rape-elimination-act.

172.   DHS takes any alleged incident of sexual abuse in immigration detention centers very seriously and takes steps to ensure that such incidents under its jurisdiction are investigated aggressively and completely. Consistent with the President's Memorandum and an amendment to PREA included in the Violence Against Women Reauthorization Act of 2013 (VAWA 2013), 42 U.S.C. 15607(c), on December 19, 2012, DHS published a notice of proposed rulemaking entitled "Standards to Prevent, Detect, and Respond to Sexual Abuse and Assault in Confinement Facilities." 77 Fed. Reg. 75300. The proposed standards would achieve the goals of prevention, detection, and response to sexual abuse and assault in covered confinement facilities by requiring prevention planning; prompt and coordinated response and intervention; training and education for staff, contractors, volunteers, and detainees; appropriate treatment for victims; procedures for investigation, discipline and prosecution of perpetrators; data collection and review for corrective action; and audits for compliance with the standards. In addition, the proposed standards would require regular audits of each immigration detention facility and holding facility that houses detainees overnight to assess compliance with the proposed standards. The open comment period ended on February 26, 2013.

173.   In addition to its rulemaking efforts, DHS continues to administer and implement other appropriate measures to prevent sexual violence in its detention facilities. ICE, the DHS

61

component primarily responsible for immigration detention facilities, has a zero tolerance policy for sexual assault and abuse in all of its facilities. Following the 2009 release of NPREC's recommendations, ICE and CRCL conducted a comprehensive review of the Commission's recommendations and the existing detention standard to incorporate the NPREC recommendations to the fullest extent possible. In May 2012, ICE issued a Directive on Sexual Abuse and Assault Prevention and Intervention, establishing agency-wide policy and procedures for addressing sexual abuse or assault of individuals in ICE custody and delineating the duties of agency employees for timely reporting, coordinated response, investigation, and effective monitoring of such incidents. Pursuant to this Directive, in July 2012 ICE appointed an agency-wide Prevention of Sexual Assault (PSA) Coordinator to develop, implement, and oversee agency efforts related to sexual abuse and assault prevention and intervention. The PSA Coordinator is responsible for working with other ICE entities to ensure an effective agency response to allegations of sexual abuse and assault.

174.   The ICE Performance-Based National Detention Standards (PBNDS) contain robust safeguards against sexual abuse or assault of detainees. These standards address prevention and intervention strategies; methods for reporting, responding to, and investigating incidents of sexual abuse or assault in coordination with criminal law enforcement entities; and requirements for screening, data monitoring, staff training and detainee education, and protection and appropriate housing for victims. ICE seeks to ensure compliance with its national standards through an aggressive annual inspections program, as discussed in the 2011 ICCPR Report ¶¶ 242-243, incorporated herein by reference.

175.   On February 10, 2013, DoD issued Directive-type Memorandum 13-002, "Department of Defense Implementation of the Prison Rape Elimination Act (PREA)", DTM 13-002. The memorandum establishes policy for DoD correctional facilities, stating that DoD is "committed to work diligently to prevent, detect, and respond to prison rape." Among other things, it directs that "[a]ll allegations of sexual assault, regardless of severity or merit, will be immediately reported to the appropriate Military Criminal Investigation Organization for investigation," and that "the Military Departments will rapidly develop and implement necessary rules and procedures to satisfy the requirements of PREA with strict enforcement measures and universally high standards."

Response to issues raised in Question 32(b).

176.   DOJ/BJS is the primary source for criminal justice statistics. PREA § 4 requires BJS "to carry out, for each calendar year, a comprehensive statistical review and analysis of the incidence and effects of prison rape." In fulfilling this mandate, BJS issues reports on sexual victimization of prisoners, including sexual conduct involving correctional staff as well as that involving other inmates. For adult inmates, BJS produces separate reports based on (1) information obtained from reporting by inmates and (2) information reported by correctional authorities in adult facilities. Facilities covered by these two reports include state and federal prisons, jails, and special confinement facilities (operated by ICE, Indian tribes, or the U.S. Armed Services). In May 2012 BJS for the first time supplemented this information in a report based on information from former state prisoners. For juvenile inmates, BJS prepares reports from information reported by youth in juvenile facilities. BJS also posts an annual summary of all of its PREA-related reports; the most recent, PREA Data Collection Activities, 2012, is available at www.bjs.gov/content/pub/pdf/pdca12.pdf. All PREA-related BJS reports are available at www.bjs.gov/index.cfm?ty=pbtp&tid=20&sid=0&iid=0&sortby=dt. A discussion of the findings on prevalence in recent reports is provided in the Annex A to this Report.

177.   In addition, the U.S. Office of Justice Programs Review Panel on Prison Rape established under PREA holds public hearings based on the BJS reports to identify the common characteristics of (1) sexual predators and victims, (2) correctional institutions with a low prevalence of sexual victimization, and (3) correctional institutions with a high prevalence of sexual victimization, and to make recommendations and identify topics for further study. Panel reports from 2010 on juvenile correctional facilities and 2012 on adult facilities are available at www.ojp.usdoj.gov/reviewpanel/reviewpanel.htm.

Response to issues raised in Question 32(c).

178.   The United States takes all allegations of sexual violence and other violence in detention centers seriously, whether or not they amount to torture or cruel, inhuman or degrading treatment or punishment. The final DOJ PREA regulations contain extensive requirements aimed at ensuring that all allegations of sexual abuse in detention centers are thoroughly investigated and referred to the proper authorities, where appropriate. See, e.g., 28 C.F.R. 115.22(a), 115.71. To the extent that a correctional agency is responsible for investigating allegations of sexual abuse, the agency must follow a uniform evidence protocol that maximizes the potential for obtaining

usable physical evidence for administrative proceedings and criminal prosecutions. The agency must offer victims no-cost access to forensic medical examinations where evidentiary or medically appropriate. In addition, the agency must attempt to make available a victim advocate from a rape crisis center, or provide similar services through qualified staff or other community-based organization. 28 C.F.R. 115.21, 115.121, 115.221. 115.321. The regulations require multiple internal ways for inmates to report sexual abuse, at least one external reporting avenue, a method for receipt of third-party reports, and a requirement for staff to report any knowledge, suspicion, or information regarding an incident of sexual abuse or sexual harassment that occurs in a detention center. See, e.g., 28 C.F.R. 115.51, 115.54, 115.61.

179.   As indicated in response to Question 32(b), in addition to data collected confidentially from inmates, BJS also collects data on sexual victimization from adult facility correctional officers based on official records in the relatively small number of cases in which an inmate reports a violation to authorities. In the most recent report by correctional authorities, covering 2007-2008, in substantiated cases of sexual victimization by prison staff (consisting of sexual misconduct or sexual harassment[4]) staff members were arrested and referred for prosecution, or received other sanctions (e.g., reprimand and demotion). Substantiated incidents of inmate-on-inmate sexual victimization result in disciplinary sanctions, legal action, placement in higher custody within the same facility, loss of privileges, or transfer to another facility. For further information, see Bureau of Justice Statistics, Sexual Victimization Reported by Adult Correctional Authorities, 2007-2008 (January 2011), available at http://bjs.ojp.usdoj.gov/content/pub/pdf/svraca0708.pdf. Examples of suits for declaratory or equitable relief are provided in the 2011 ICCPR Report ¶ 224, incorporated herein by reference.

180.   DHS/ICE is committed to preventing and responding aggressively and swiftly to sexual assault in immigration detention. ICE detainees may report a sexual abuse or assault incident to

---

[4] Staff sexual misconduct is defined by BJS as including "any sexual behavior or act directed toward an inmate by staff, including romantic relationships. Such acts include intentional touching of the genitalia, anus, groin, breast, inner thigh, or buttocks with the intent to abuse, arouse, or gratify sexual desire; or completed, attempted, threatened, or requested sexual acts; or occurrences of indecent exposure, invasion of privacy, or staff voyeurism for sexual gratification."

Staff sexual harassment is defined by BJS to include repeated statements or comments of a sexual nature to an inmate by staff. Such statements include demeaning references to an inmate's sex or derogatory comments about his or her body or clothing; or repeated profane or obscene language or gestures."

multiple oversight entities, including DHS/OIG, the ICE/OPR Joint Intake Center, DHS/CRCL, the local ICE Field Office, and facility staff. ICE policy ensures that each such allegation is promptly investigated, whether by ICE itself, facility staff, or local law enforcement. In addition, ICE is undertaking various measures to improve these reporting mechanisms, including by coordinating with DHS/OIG to expedite the sharing of incident reports between OIG and OPR, and improving communications between ICE headquarters and field offices. DHS/CRCL also investigates allegations of inadequate conditions of detention for ICE detainees. Examples of such investigations are available in the 2011 ICCPR Report ¶ 225, incorporated herein by reference.

181.   Policies and programs to support the reporting of acts of violence in detention centers are addressed in response to Questions 32(a) and (b).

Response to issues raised in Question 32(d) and on impact and effectiveness.
182.   Avenues for pursuing redress are discussed in response to Questions 27 and 28. Illustrative cases demonstrate the ability of victims of sexual violence to obtain redress in the United States. For example:

> In January 2011, the U.S. Supreme Court reinstated a $625,000 jury verdict awarded to a female inmate against Ohio prison officials for failure to provide reasonable protection from violence while in custody based on allegations of sexual assault while incarcerated. Ortiz v. Jordan, 131 S. Ct. 884 (2011).

> In June 2010, the New York State Department of Correctional Services agreed to pay a $300,000 settlement to Stephen Lewis, a prisoner at the Arthur Kill Correctional Facility who accused a prison guard of sexually assaulting him in violation of the Eighth Amendment's prohibition of cruel and unusual punishment. Lewis v. Fischer, No. 08-CV-3027 (E.D.N.Y. 2010).

183.   In July 2009, the state of Michigan agreed to pay a $100 million settlement in a class-action brought by more than 500 female prisoners who alleged that they had been sexually assaulted by prison guards. Neal v. Michigan Department of Corrections; Anderson v. Michigan Department of Corrections.

184. A 2009 DOJ/OIG report on penalties under federal law for staff sexual abuse of federal prisoners with use or threat of force found that since 2006 when new laws changed misdemeanor sexual abuse crimes to felony crimes, the percentage of cases accepted for prosecution had increased from 37 percent to 49 percent – a 12 percent increase. The percentage of convictions had also increased from 30 percent to 78 percent. Of 90 prosecutions, 83 had resulted in convictions or guilty pleas; in addition, there had been one acquittal and six dismissals. The DOJ/OIG report is available at www.justice.gov/oig/reports/plus/e0904.pdf.

185. DHS continues to implement and improve the policies described above as part of its broader detention reform efforts. Although it is working toward this goal, DHS is not yet able to quantify the impact of these measures.

33. In light of the Committee's previous concluding observations, please elaborate on the measures adopted by the State party to ensure that women in detention are treated in conformity with international standards, as well as on the implementation of these measures (para. 33). Furthermore, please provide information on the impact and effectiveness of these measures in reducing cases of ill-treatment of detained women.

186. The final DOJ PREA regulations, discussed in response to Question 32(a), include several protections specifically aimed at protecting women in detention. These include prohibiting cross-gender pat searches, strip searches, and cavity searches of both adult women and juveniles, while specifically mandating that women's access to programming and out-of-cell opportunities must not be restricted to comply with these requirements. 28 C.F.R. §§ 115.15, 115.115, 115.215, 115.315. The standards also require facilities to implement policies and procedures that enable inmates to shower, perform bodily functions, and change clothing without nonmedical staff of the opposite gender viewing their breasts, buttocks, or genitalia, except in exigent circumstances or when such viewing is incidental to routine cell checks. Facilities also must require staff of the opposite gender to announce their presence when entering an inmate housing unit. In addition to removing some potential opportunities for abuse, these standards attempt to address the possibility that an inmate who has experienced prior sexual abuse could experience cross-gender searches or viewing as particularly traumatizing, even if the officers conduct themselves properly. Female inmates are especially vulnerable owing to their disproportionate likelihood of having previously suffered abuse.

187.   DOJ/BOP staff members are trained to respect all inmates' safety, dignity, and privacy, and procedures exist for investigation of complaints and disciplinary action, including criminal prosecution, against staff who violate applicable laws and regulations. Upon hiring, staff members are trained on the Standards of Employee Conduct. Refresher training is mandatory on an annual basis. All staff members assigned to work at female institutions are required to complete a training course regarding their work with female offenders. Upon arrival at the institution, all federal inmates are also trained on the agency's zero-tolerance policy on sexual abuse and the complaint procedures.

188.   DOJ protects the rights of women who are incarcerated in facilities run by or for states through its enforcement of the Civil Rights of Institutionalized Persons Act (CRIPA) and the Violent Crime Control and Law Enforcement Act of 1994 discussed in response to Question 42. DOJ has successfully brought actions to protect female prisoners from sexual misconduct and invasion of privacy by male prison staff.

189.   DHS/ICE also has recently taken steps to enhance its current policy concerning treatment of female inmates. In facilities subject to DHS/ICE's PBNDS 2011 standards, staff of the opposite sex are required to announce their presence prior to entering housing units as is generally required in the DOJ detention context (see PBNDS 2011 Standard 2.11 "Sexual Abuse and Assault Prevention and Intervention"); a single officer is prohibited from transporting a single detainee of the opposite sex; and facility staff are prohibited from having unmonitored access (either through direct supervision or video surveillance) to detainees of the opposite sex (see PBNDS 2011 Standard 1.3 "Transportation (By Land)"). PBNDS 2011 also incorporates a new standard on Women's Medical Care to ensure the appropriate delivery of necessary medical and mental health services to female detainees (see PBNDS 2011 Standard 4.4 "Medical Care (Women)"). Information on DHS/ICE Health Services Corps (IHSC) initiatives, including women's health initiatives, is available in the 2011 ICCPR Report ¶ 240, incorporated herein by reference.

190.   In ¶ 33 of its 2006 Concluding Observations, the Committee specifically asked about shackling of women detainees in childbirth. Both the federal and some state governments have

announced policy changes that improve the standards for treatment of women during labor and delivery.

191.   The American Correctional Association (ACA), which certifies and accredits both state and federal correctional departments (including DOJ/BOP) based on nationally published standards, prohibits the use of restraints on pregnant inmates. DOJ/BOP announced in October 2008 that it would no longer engage in the practice of shackling pregnant women during transportation, labor and delivery, except in the most extreme circumstances, as sort forth in its Escorted Trips policy (5538.05). Some states are also adopting similar rules. The ACA standard and accompanying comment, and its implementation by states and the federal government are discussed in the 2011 ICCPR Report ¶¶ 231-233 and 676, incorporated herein by reference.

192.   DHS/ICE has also adopted policies prohibiting the use of restraints on pregnant women and women in post-delivery recuperation absent truly extraordinary circumstances that render restraints absolutely necessary, and outright prohibiting the use of restraints on women in active labor or delivery. The current PBNDS 2011 include specific provisions for limited situations in which physical restraint is appropriate. Although there are no reported cases where this has occurred, ICE policy would only allow the restraint of a pregnant detainee under the following rare and highly unlikely circumstances: (1) a medical officer has directed the use of restraints for medical reasons; (2) credible, reasonable grounds exist to believe the detainee presents an immediate and serious threat of hurting herself, staff or others; or (3) reasonable grounds exist to believe the detainee presents an immediate and credible risk of escape that cannot be reasonably minimized through any other method. The standards also contain requirements for utilization of the safest and least restrictive methods of restraint where their use is necessary.

34. Please provide updated information on steps taken to address the concern about the conditions of detention of children, in particular about the fact that they may not be completely segregated from adults and the use of excessive force in juvenile prisons (para. 34). Please provide information on the impact and effectiveness of these measures in improving detention of children. Furthermore, please provide information on the status and content of the draft legislation Juvenile Justice and Delinquency Prevention Reauthorization Act of 2009, which would reform the juvenile justice system.

193.   The federal Juvenile Justice and Delinquency Prevention Act (JJDPA) requires states participating in federal juvenile justice grant programs to implement policies prohibiting contact

between adult inmates and detained juvenile offenders in order to be eligible to receive federal funding under the JJDPA. 42 U.S.C. 5633. Subject to specified narrow exceptions, juveniles charged with or adjudicated for offenses applicable only to minors may not be securely detained even in juvenile facilities, and no juveniles may be detained or confined in an adult jail or lockup or be held in any institution in which they have sight or sound contact with adult inmates. The PREA regulations, 28 C.F.R. 115.14, provide further significant protections for youth in juvenile and adult facilities, and include a financial penalty for those states that do not comply with PREA.

194.   In addition, within the federal system, 18 U.S.C. 5039 requires that no juvenile committed to the custody of the Attorney General whether pursuant to an adjudication of delinquency or conviction for an offense, may be placed or retained in an adult jail or correctional institution in which he or she has regular contact with adults incarcerated because they have been convicted of a crime or are awaiting trial on criminal charges. The statute further provides that whenever possible, the Attorney General shall commit a juvenile to a foster home or community-based facility located in or near his home community.

195.   DOJ/OJJDP launched a National Center for Youth in Custody in October 2011. This national clearinghouse makes available policy guidance and access to effective practice literature in addition to providing no-cost training and technical assistance on-site to facilities wishing to improve conditions of confinement.

196.   As discussed in response to Question 42, DOJ/CRT investigates conditions in state prisons and jails and state juvenile correction and detention facilities pursuant to the Civil Rights of Institutionalized Persons Act, CRIPA, 42 U.S.C. 1997 et seq. Where conditions in those facilities warrant enforcement, DOJ institutes civil law enforcement actions under CRIPA or section 14141. Since October 2005, pursuant to CRIPA, DOJ/CRT has authorized 8 investigations of 29 juvenile detention facilities. Examples of investigations are provided in the 2011 ICCPR Report ¶ 224, incorporated herein by reference.

197.   In the immigration custody context, the Office of Refugee Resettlement (ORR) within the Department of Health and Human Services (HHS) is responsible for the care and custody of

unaccompanied alien children.[5] The William Wilberforce Trafficking Victims Protection Reauthorization Act of 2008 requires DHS and other federal agencies to notify HHS within 48 hours of the apprehension or discovery of an unaccompanied alien child or if there is any claim or suspicion that an alien in the agency's custody is under 18 years of age and, except in exceptional circumstances, to transfer custody of all unaccompanied alien children to HHS within 72 hours. See 8 U.S.C. 2343(b).

198.   While unaccompanied alien children are in DHS custody, ICE and CBP personnel ensure that the needs of this vulnerable population are addressed promptly, including by immediately segregating children from unrelated adults.

199.   ICE maintains the Berks Family Residential Center (BFRC), a small facility in which family units (typically a parent or legal guardian and at least one child under the age of 18 years) may be detained pending the completion of immigration proceedings. The BFRC environment empowers parents to continue to be responsible for their children, including for their supervision and discipline. Corporal punishment, however, is not permitted at BFRC.

200.   Information concerning detention of juveniles under the law of armed conflict is provided in response to Question 38.

201.   Concerning the Committee's request for information on the Juvenile Justice and Delinquency Prevention Reauthorization Act of 2009, in August 2010, the Senate Committee on the Judiciary reported out that legislation as Bill S. 678 to the full Senate. The bill was not, however, enacted into law. DOJ strongly supported the JDDPA reauthorization bill. In a letter to Senator Patrick Leahy, Chairman of the Committee on the Judiciary, dated April 15, 2010, DOJ stated that "supporting and improving the juvenile justice system and preventing youth violence and delinquency are among the Attorney General's top priorities." The letter stated that the bill would advance these goals through measures that provide juveniles with access to high-quality, effective juvenile justice and delinquency prevention programs and protect them from harmful

---

[5] An unaccompanied alien child is defined as a child who "(A) has no lawful immigration status in the United States; (B) has not attained 18 years of age; and (C) with respect to whom (i) there is no parent or legal guardian in the United States; or (ii) no parent or legal guardian in the United States available to provide care and physical custody." 6 U.S.C. 279(g)(2).

conditions of confinement. The current Congress has not reintroduced legislation reauthorizing the JJDPA.

35. Please describe steps taken to prohibit the sentencing of juveniles to life imprisonment without the possibility of parole, as recommended by the Committee in its previous concluding observations (para. 34).

202.   In 2010 the U.S. Supreme Court held that the Eighth Amendment prohibits the sentencing of a juvenile offender to life in prison without parole for a non-homicide-related crime, as such a sentence would constitute cruel and unusual punishment. Graham v. Florida, 130 S. Ct. 2011 (2010). In 2012 the Court held in a murder case that mandatory life without parole for those under age 18 at the time of their crime violates the Eighth Amendment's prohibition on cruel and unusual punishment. Miller v. Alabama, 132 S.Ct. 2455 (2012). This issue is also addressed in the 2011 ICCPR Report ¶¶ 212 and 679 and 2013 CERD Report ¶ 71, incorporated herein by reference.

36. Please indicate if the State party has reviewed the use of electroshock devices and regulated their use, restricting it to substitution for lethal weapons, as recommended by the Committee in its previous concluding observations (para. 35). Are such devices still used to restrain persons in custody?

203.   Courts have found that, under the Fourth Amendment of the U. S. Constitution, deadly force "may not be used unless it is necessary to prevent the escape and the officer has probable cause to believe that the suspect poses a significant threat of death or serious physical injury to the officer or others," Tennessee v. Garner, 471 U.S. 1, 3 (1985), and all uses of force, whether lethal or non-lethal, must be "'objectively reasonable' in light of the facts and circumstances confronting" the officer. Graham v. Connor, 490 U.S. 386, 397 (1989). The determination of whether use of an Electro-Muscular-Disruption (EMD) device is justifiable under this standard requires balancing the amount of force applied against the need for that force. Meredith v. Erath, 342 F.3d 1057, 1061 (9th Cir. 2001). Many factors must be taken into account in making this determination, but one important factor is the vulnerability of the person against whom such force is directed. U.S. federal courts have held that the use of electroshock devices by law enforcement officers constitutes an intermediate, significant level of force that, though considered non-lethal, must be justified by a government interest that compels the employment of such force. Bryan v. MacPherson, 630 F.3d 805, 826 (9th Cir. 2010). Ultimately, the most

important factor in determining whether the use of such force is justified is whether an individual poses an "immediate threat to the safety of the officers or others." Id. DOJ/CRT has enforced the limitations on the use of electroshock devices, for instance in 2010 by filing a complaint in intervention pursuant to 42 U.S.C. 14141 against the Franklin County Sheriff's Office in Columbus, Ohio. Shreve v. Franklin County, Ohio, No. 2:10-cv-244 (S.D. Ohio, filed Nov. 3, 2010).

204.   DOJ takes very seriously any resort to use of force during law enforcement operations, including the use of EMDs. In regards to restraining persons in custody, the sole electroshock device used by DOJ/BOP is an electronic custody control belt. The device is used during community transport only after determining that an inmate requires greater security than is afforded through conventional restraints, and the inmate has no medical condition precluding its use. Activation of the device is only authorized in circumstances where deadly force is otherwise justified, i.e., to prevent escape and there is a significant threat of death or serious bodily injury and any such activation must be properly reviewed, documented and reported.

205.   DOJ's National Institute of Justice has been conducting a review of instances in which individuals died after law enforcement officers used EMDs to subdue them. This impartial and comprehensive research should lead to a better understanding regarding any potential safety risks involving the use of EMD devices. The Department also works with local police agencies and associations and correctional facility personnel to assist the local law enforcement agencies in their policy development regarding the use of EMD devices.

206.   DHS/ICE has reviewed the EMD devices currently available to law enforcement agencies and has not authorized any for use by ICE personnel. Authorized CBP officers and agents may use an EMD as an intermediate force device when such use would be objectively reasonable based on the perspective of a similarly-situated CBP officer or agent. The 2009 CBP EMD policy dictates that such devices may only be used on subjects who, at a minimum, demonstrate active resistance and only to the extent reasonably necessary to control and secure a resistant subject, protect themselves or others from bodily harm, make an arrest, prevent an escape, and/or enforce compliance with a lawful order. The devices may only be used by personnel who have successfully completed an EMD training course approved by CBP's Use of Force Policy

72

Division consisting of at least eight hours of instruction and an annual four-hour refresher course. CBP EMD policy specifically provides that the devices should not be used on small children, the elderly, pregnant women or persons with low body mass index; or on a subject who is near known flammable materials, on elevated surfaces, operating a conveyance, adjacent to traffic, in water sufficient to drown or running on hard surfaces (e.g., concrete or asphalt); or handcuffed. Any person(s) exposed to such a device by CBP personnel are promptly referred to an emergency medical technician for evaluation.

207.   Following any incident that results in the discharge of an EMD, CBP personnel must report the incident. Wherever practicable, CBP personnel should photograph or videotape any marks or injuries resulting from the use of an ECD. If the marks or alleged injuries to be documented are on a private portion of the subject's body, CBP personnel make reasonable efforts to ensure privacy before the documentation is recorded, including but not limited to documentation by an officer/agent of the same gender as the subject.

37. Please describe steps taken to improve the extremely harsh regime imposed on detainees in "super-maximum security prisons", in particular the practice of prolonged isolation.

208.   The U.S. Constitution, along with federal and state laws, establishes standards of care to which all inmates are entitled, which are consistent with the U.S. obligations as a party to the CAT and which seek to promote the basic principles underlying the non-binding recommendations with respect to good principles and practices set forth in the UN Standard Minimum Rules for the Treatment of Prisoners.

209.   U.S. courts have interpreted the Eighth and Fourteenth Amendments of the U.S. Constitution as prohibiting the use of solitary confinement under certain circumstances, especially with regard to inmates with serious mental illness or for juvenile detainees.[6] Inmates

---

[6] Specifically, under the Eighth Amendment's prohibition against "cruel and unusual punishments," correctional facility administrators may not subject inmates to solitary confinement with deliberate indifference to the resulting serious harms, including suicides, suicide attempts, and serious self-injury. See Farmer v. Brennan, 511 U.S. 825, 843 (1970); see also, e.g., Madrid v. Gomez, 889 F. Supp. 1146, 1265 (N.D. Cal. 1995) (using prolonged solitary confinement on prisoners with serious mental illness can be "the mental equivalent of putting an asthmatic in a place with little air to breathe"). Under the Fourteenth Amendment's Due Process Clause, prisoners have a protected liberty interest in avoiding certain types of solitary confinement. Wilkinson v. Austin, 545 U.S. 209, 22e-224 (2005).

cannot be subjected to solitary confinement absent an administrative hearing and other procedures protective of their right to due process.

210.   The Americans with Disabilities Act of 1990 (ADA) and the Rehabilitation Act of 1973 (Rehabilitation Act) restrict and regulate the use of solitary confinement for persons with disabilities. Title II of the ADA, 42 U.S.C. 12132, applies to state actors, while the Rehabilitation Act applies to federal correctional facilities and correctional facilities receiving funds from the federal government. Both statutes prohibit the use of solitary confinement in a manner that discriminates on the basis of disability instead of making reasonable modifications to provide persons with disabilities access to services, programs, and activities, including mental health services. See Pa. Dep't of Corr. v. Yeskey, 524 U.S. 206, 210 (1998).

211.   PREA restricts the use of solitary confinement for juvenile inmates and inmates who are the victims of sexual violence. Under implementing regulations, juveniles "may be isolated from others only as a last resort when less restrictive measures are inadequate to keep them and other residents safe, and then only until an alternative means of keeping all residents safe can be arranged." 28 C.F.R. 115.342. The regulations also set time limits and other limitations on the use of solitary confinement on juvenile inmates. With regard to adult inmates at high risk for sexual victimization, the regulations establish conditions on placement in segregated housing and provide that if such inmates are placed in segregated housing, they are to have access to programs, education, work opportunities, and other services to the extent possible. 28 C.F.R. 115.43(a)-(b).

212.   DOJ/CRT investigates allegations of misuse of solitary confinement in violation of the constitutional and statutory provisions discussed above. Some of these laws and standards extend to private correctional facilities. DOJ/CRT recently settled a case arising from an investigation of a jail in Tennessee, requiring the facility to end its practice of using solitary confinement as an alternative to meaningful treatment of those with mental illness, www.justice.gov/crt/about/spl. In May 2013, DOJ/CRT issued a report finding that the Pennsylvania Department of Correction's use of prolonged solitary confinement on prisoners with serious mental illness and intellectual disabilities at the State Correctional Institution in Cresson violates the Eighth Amendment and federal and state law. DOJ/CRT expanded its investigation to Pennsylvania's

entire prison system to determine whether similar practices exist in other correctional facilities, www.justice.gov/opa/pr/2013/May/13-crt-631.html and www.justice.gov/crt/about/spl/findsettle.php#corrections.

213.   DOJ/BOP meets its constitutional and statutory mandates by confining inmates in prisons and community-based facilities that are safe, humane, and appropriately secure. For certain violent inmates, maximum security facilities may be necessary, inter alia, to protect the safety of the community at large and of other members of the prison population.

214.   As stated in a letter of November 30, 2011, responding to a request from the Special Rapporteur on Torture and Other Cruel, Inhuman or Degrading Treatment or Punishment, "[t]here is no systematic use of solitary confinement in the United States." Noting that the Special Rapporteur had cited the U.S. Penitentiary, Administrative Maximum (ADX) facility as an example of a facility that places inmates in solitary confinement, the letter provided information including the following:

> Security requirements at the ADX mandate restrictive procedures for movement of inmates and physical interaction with staff. For security reasons, inmates in General Population spend most of their day in individual cells. They are not deprived, however, of human interaction. Inmates can speak with (but not touch) one another in the recreation yards, and can communicate with the inmates housed on either side of their cells. The Warden, Associate Wardens, Captain, and Department Heads perform weekly rounds so they can visit with each inmate. Correctional Officers perform regular rounds throughout all three shifts on a daily basis. A member of an inmate's Unit Team visits him every day, Monday through Friday, except on holidays. Inmates receive regular visits from medical staff, education staff, religious services staff, and mental health staff, and upon request if needed. In addition, General Population inmates are permitted five non-contact social visits per month and two fifteen-minute phone calls. Inmates in less restrictive housing units are permitted even more social visits and phone calls. Inmates can also send and receive personal correspondence.

215.   In certain circumstances, due process hearings must be afforded to prisoners before a maximum security assignment may be imposed. The U.S. Supreme Court has held that a 30-day

period of disciplinary segregation of prisoners from the general population does not give rise to a liberty interest that would require a full due process hearing prior to imposition of the punishment, although the Court left open the possibility that due process protections would be implicated if the confinement was "atypical and significant." Sandin v. Conner, 515 U.S. 472 (1995). In 2005 the Supreme Court assessed whether confinement to a "Supermax" maximum security prison facility in Ohio constituted an "atypical and significant hardship" giving rise to a liberty interest under the Sandin standard, Wilkinson v. Austin, 545 U.S. 209 (2005). The Court determined that maximum security placement does constitute an "atypical and significant" hardship because such placement cuts off almost all human contact, is indefinite and reviewed only annually (as opposed to the 30-day period involved in Sandin), and disqualifies an otherwise eligible inmate for consideration for parole. The Court found that the state of Ohio's revised policy for maximum security assignment provided a sufficient level of due process to meet the constitutional standard because, among other things, it established multiple levels of review, with the process terminating if any level rejected the assignment, provided notice and opportunity for rebuttal, and provided for a placement review within 30 days of initial assignment.

38. Please provide information on steps taken to address the reports of inhumane conditions at Guantánamo Bay, in particular experienced by children, including by allowing phone calls with family members and providing detainees with educational opportunities and materials. Information should be provided on the impact and effectiveness of these measures in improving the detention conditions at Guantánamo Bay.

216.   The conditions of detention at Guantanamo meet or exceed all U.S. obligations under international law. No individuals currently detained at Guantanamo are juveniles. Omar Khadr, who was 16 years old when he was transferred to Guantanamo, pleaded guilty before a military commission as discussed in ¶ 55 and was sentenced pursuant to a pre-trial agreement to eight years imprisonment. On September 29, 2012, he was transferred to Canada to serve the remainder of his sentence.

217.   The United States recognizes the often difficult and unfortunate circumstances of young detainees. If the United States detains a juvenile under the law of armed conflict, the United States goes to great lengths to attend to the special needs of the juvenile while in detention. The United States has special procedures in place to evaluate detainees medically, to determine their

ages, to provide for detention facilities and treatment appropriate for their ages, to provide them with safe and humane care and custody, including such special medical, dental, physical and psychological care as might be required under the circumstances, and provides, at a minimum, telephone and video contact with their families when possible.

218. As to treatment of the detainee population at Guantanamo generally, in E.O. 13492, President Obama directed the Secretary of Defense to undertake a comprehensive review of the conditions of confinement to assess compliance with Common Article 3 of the Geneva Conventions. Admiral Patrick Walsh, Vice Chief of Naval Operations, assembled a team of experts from throughout DoD to conduct an independent assessment that considered all aspects of detention operations and facilities at Guantanamo. The DoD review found that "the conditions of confinement in Guantanamo are in conformity with Common Article 3 of the Geneva Conventions" and that they "also meet the directive requirements of Common Article 3 of the Geneva Conventions."[7] The review team noted "that the chain of command responsible for the detention mission at Guantanamo seeks to go beyond a minimalist approach to compliance with Common Article 3, and endeavors to enhance conditions in a manner as humane as possible consistent with security concerns." The Joint Task Force at Guantanamo continually reviews its operations to ensure humane treatment and consistency with the Geneva Conventions and makes improvements wherever possible for the comfort of detainees and the safety of the guard force.

219. The majority of Guantanamo detainees generally are housed in communal living facilities, where they are able to eat, sleep, and live with others. Detainees are provided three meals per day that meet religious dietary requirements – they are prepared halal – and provided with menu options that add up to about 4,500 calories per day. Detainees on a hunger strike who are medically evaluated as needing nourishment are nourished in accordance with procedures similar to those applicable to inmates in federal prison. Detainees are offered special meals for feast celebrations, and the guard force adjusts their meal schedule during Ramadan so that detainees can properly fast during the daylight hours. Detainees also have the opportunity to engage in daily prayer and worship. A copy of the Koran is offered to each detainee in his native

---

[7] Review of Department Compliance with President's Executive Order on Detainee Conditions of Confinement, February 2009 [hereinafter the Walsh Report], available at www.defense.gov/pubs/pdfs/REVIEW_OF_DEPARTMENT_COMPLIANCE_WITH_PRESIDENTS_EXECUTIV E_ORDER_ON_DETAINEE_CONDITIONS_OF_CONFINEMENTa.pdf

language. Detainees receive prayer beads, prayer rugs, and prayer caps, and the Muslim call to prayer is played over camp loudspeakers five times a day. Once the call to prayer sounds, detainees receive 20 minutes of uninterrupted time to practice their faith. The guards strive to ensure that detainees are not interrupted during prayer times. Throughout the detention camps, stenciled arrows pointing in the direction of Mecca are displayed for prayer.

220.   The detention camps provide opportunities for outdoor recreation, which may include basketball and soccer. Indoor recreation in certain facilities includes reading, satellite television, video games, board games, and movies on DVD. The detainee library, staffed by a full time librarian, has thousands of books, magazines, and DVDs, and these materials are distributed to the detainees on at least a weekly basis. Books range from picture books to doctoral-level reading.

221.   Over the past few years, the staff at Guantanamo has added classes for the detainees, including art, language, humanities, and life skills. These classes give detainees a form of intellectual stimulation and have aided some in transitioning to lives after their transfer home or to a third country.

222.   The medical staff at Guantanamo provides the detainees with quality care on the same level as that which U.S. service members receive while on base. There is a dedicated medical facility, including dental and mental health practitioners, with equipment and an expert staff of more than 100 medical personnel. The detainee hospital has 17 beds, an operating room, a fully stocked pharmacy, a physical therapy area, optometry, radiology, and dental suites. There is one licensed care provider for every 57 detainees – by contrast, in the United States the provider to patient ratio is one care provider for every 390 patients. Detainees at Guantanamo have received immunizations.

223.   DoD, with the assistance of the ICRC, has established a video-teleconference program through which many detainees are able to see and speak with their family members. For those without the ability to connect via video, most are able to communicate with their families via telephone. Detainees are also able to send and receive an unlimited amount of mail. Camp authorities at Guantanamo are keenly aware of the need to ensure detainees are not linguistically

isolated, and they make sure that detainees are held in close proximity to those who speak their language.

39. Please inform the Committee of steps taken to address the reports of inconsistent and inadequate medical care for immigrant women held by United States Immigration and Customs Enforcement detention system and for HIV-positive immigration detainees.

224. As part of its ongoing immigration detention reform programs, DHS has significantly improved health services for persons in its custody. ICE Health Services Corps (IHSC) provides health care to immigration detainees, including women and those detainees identified as HIV-positive, in accordance with community-based standards, standards of the ACA and the National Commission on Correctional Health Care (NCCHC), and the ICE PBNDS, discussed in response to Question 33. Further, PBNDS 2011 incorporates a new standard more specifically outlining requirements for appropriate and consistent care of women's health issues as a matter of policy, and requiring that detainees diagnosed with HIV/AIDS receive medical care consistent with national recommendations and guidelines disseminated through the U.S. Department of Health and Human Services, the Centers for Disease Control and the Infectious Diseases Society of America. IHSC has also published a "Patient Bill of Rights" informing patients of their entitlements and responsibilities, and has an active medical grievance mechanism to respond to detainee concerns regarding health care, including allegations specific to female medical needs. Further information on IHSC is provided in the 2011 ICCPR Report ¶ 240 incorporated herein by reference.

225. DHS/CRCL investigates complaints alleging inappropriate or inadequate medical care at immigration detention facilities. CRCL has investigated complaints alleging problems with medical care for HIV-positive detainees and has assisted HIV-positive detainees to ensure that they receive timely and appropriate HIV medication and chronic care follow-up services. Investigations include onsite fact-finding at immigration detention facilities, during which CRCL staff and experts in both medical and mental health care evaluate whether the medical care provided at a facility satisfies both national immigration detention standards and professional standards such as those published by the NCCHC. In completing its investigations, CRCL issues specific recommendations to leadership at ICE in order to improve any deficiencies found or concerns raised during the investigation.

40. Please describe steps taken to end the practice of corporal punishment in schools, in particular of mentally and/or physically disabled students.

226.   In the United States, the way in which schools and school districts discipline their students is largely a matter of state and local law and practice. For the past thirty years, there has been a significant trend away from corporal punishment. In the late 1970s, only two of the 50 states prohibited corporal punishment in schools. Currently 31 states and the District of Columbia prohibit corporal punishment in schools and even in states where it is not prohibited, many school districts and schools do not permit its use.

227.   U.S. courts have recognized and enforced a constitutionally protected right of students to be free from corporal punishment that is excessive or arbitrary under the Due Process clause of the Fifth and Fourteenth Amendments. Kirkland v. Greene County Board of Education, 347 F.3d 903 (11th Cir. 2003); P.B. v. Koch, 96 F.3d 1298 (9th Cir. 1996); Moore v. Willis Independent School District, 233 F.3d 871 (5th Cir. 2000); Saylor v. Board of Education of Harlan County, 118 F.3d 507 (6th Cir. 1997). DOJ and the Department of Education (ED) Office for Civil Rights have ongoing investigations of discriminatory disciplinary practices involving students of color and students with disabilities. In addition, DOJ and ED are working on policy guidance to assist school districts in ensuring non-discrimination in discipline policies and practices. ED requires reporting on the use of corporal punishment in public schools by race/ethnicity, sex, disability, and limited English proficiency status as part of its expanded efforts to ensure that the administration of school discipline is non-discriminatory, http://ocrdata.ed.gov/.

228.   A discriminatory imposition of discipline on children with disabilities is prohibited under Section 504 of the Rehabilitation Act and the ADA, and is subject to the ADA's broad enforcement authorities and measures. The Individuals with Disabilities Education Act provides specific protections to eligible students with disabilities related to disciplinary actions. When ED receives a complaint alleging disability discrimination related to corporal punishment, the Department is almost always able to resolve any compliance issues voluntarily through a resolution agreement but also has recourse to administrative hearings or litigation.

229.   Many ongoing efforts support development of positive school climates and improving school discipline policies, procedures, and practices. For example, ED funds the Positive Behavioral Interventions and Supports Center (PBIS), which is designed to provide capacity-

building information and technical assistance to states, school districts and schools to identify, adopt, and sustain effective positive school-wide disciplinary practices. More than 19,000 schools across the country are implementing PBIS – frequently resulting in significant reductions in the behaviors that lead to disciplinary referrals, suspensions, and expulsions. For more information, see www.pbis.org. ED also provides technical assistance to assist state and local educational agencies for these purposes, encourages states and school districts in the use of conflict resolution techniques, and promotes the use of early intervention services.

41. Please provide information on steps taken to:

(a) Prevent and punish violence and abuse of women, in particular women belonging to racial, ethnic and national minorities. Do these measures include providing specific training for those working within the criminal justice system and raising awareness about the mechanisms and procedures provided for in national legislation on racism and discrimination?

(b) Address the report of an increase in incidences of domestic violence, rape and sexual assault (National Crime Victimization Survey, December 2008).

(c) Ensure that reports of violence against women are independently, promptly and thoroughly investigated, and that perpetrators are prosecuted and appropriately punished. Please include statistical data on the number of complaints concerning violence against women and the related investigations, prosecutions, convictions and sanctions, as well as on compensation provided to victims.

Response to issues raised in Question 41(a).

230. Protecting women from violence, whether or not it constitutes torture or cruel, inhuman or degrading treatment, is a priority for the United States. President Obama has appointed the first-ever White House Advisor on Violence Against Women to collaborate with the many federal agencies working together to end violence against women.

231. VAWA 2013, enacted March 7, 2013, was the third reauthorization of the Violence Against Women Act of 1994, a landmark law that has transformed the way that the United States responds to domestic and sexual violence. The VAWA is discussed further in the 2011 ICCPR Report ¶¶ 53-54 and 134-142, incorporated herein by reference.

232. VAWA 2013 includes crucial new provisions to improve services for victims, expand access to justice, and strengthen the prosecutorial and enforcement tools available to hold perpetrators accountable. VAWA 2013 finally closes a loophole that left many Native American women without adequate protection by providing significant new jurisdiction by tribal courts

over cases alleging abuse of Native American women on tribal lands by an attacker who is not Native American. Tribes and the federal government can better work together to address domestic violence against Native American women, who experience very high rates of assault in the United States. The law also provides funding to improve the criminal justice response to sexual assault, ensuring that victims can access the services they need to heal. VAWA 2013 will also help to build on evidence-based practices for reducing domestic violence homicides, prevent violence against children, teens, and young adults, and protect everyone – women and men, gay and straight, and children and adults of all races, ethnicities, countries of origin, and tribal affiliations.

233.   Each year, all 50 states, the District of Columbia and various U.S. territories are awarded DOJ Office for Victims of Crime grants to support community-based organizations that serve crime victims. Approximately 5,600 grants are made to domestic violence shelters, rape crisis centers, child abuse programs, and victim service units in various agencies and hospitals. On March 13, 2013, DOJ announced its first-ever Domestic Violence Homicide Prevention Demonstration Initiative grant awards – through which DOJ will distribute $2.3 million to 12 cities and counties to support innovative programs dedicated to predicting potentially lethal behavior, stopping the escalation of violence, and saving lives.

234.   As a general matter, research indicates that survivors are more inclined to seek services from organizations that are familiar with their culture, language and background. Culturally-specific community-based organizations are more likely to understand the obstacles that victims from their communities face when attempting to access services. These organizations also are better equipped to engage their communities. VAWA grant programs support the development of diverse organizations that represent underserved groups, including community- and faith-based organizations. For example, the Grants to Enhance Culturally and Linguistically Specific Services for Victims of Domestic Violence, Dating Violence, Sexual Assault and Stalking Program, created in 2005, creates a unique opportunity for targeted community-based organizations to address the critical needs of domestic violence, dating violence, sexual assault and stalking victims. In addition, the Tribal Governments Program provides funds to tribes to develop and implement governmental strategies to curtail violence against women. This funding has expanded on funding previously provided through the STOP Violence Against Indian

Women Program, which served originally as the impetus for significant changes in how tribal communities respond to the victimization of American Indian/Alaska Native women. The Tribal Governments Program funding gives tribal governments the flexibility to develop solutions appropriate for their communities. The Tribal Sexual Assault Services Program provides funds to tribes to specifically address sexual assault through the development and implementation of direct intervention and related assistance (e.g., crisis intervention, cultural advocacy, hospital accompaniment, transportation, criminal/civil justice advocacy) to American Indian/Alaska Native victims.

235.   Additional information on programs administered by DOJ/OVW, DHS, and the Department of Housing and Urban Development, is provided in the 2011 ICCPR Report ¶¶ 135-142, incorporated herein by reference.

Response to issues raised in Question 41(b).
236.   Changes made to the survey methodology used in the National Crime Victimization Survey (NCVS) in 2006 resulted in what appeared to be a significant increase in victimization rates under the heading "Violent crime: rape/sexual assault" between 2006 and 2007 in the report issued in December 2008 (Table 3). As stated in that report, analyses undertaken by DOJ/BJS and the U.S. Census Bureau established that the year-to-year 2005 to 2006 and 2006 to 2007 NCVS estimates were not comparable as a result of methodological changes introduced to the survey in 2006. In its report issued September 2009, BJS decided to exclude estimates for 2006 based on the conclusion that the 2006 findings represented a temporary anomaly in the data. The reports are available at www.bjs.gov/index.cfm?ty=pbse&sid=6.

237.   A more recent and comprehensive statistical treatment of these trends is now available. In 2012 and 2013, BJS released two reports focusing on sexual violence and intimate partner violence that present the most current findings on nonfatal and fatal violent crimes against females in the United States. Data are primarily from the National Crime Victimization Survey (NCVS), 1993 to 2010. Both reports recorded significant declines in incidence. The first report, Intimate Partner Violence, 1993-2010, focuses on intimate partner violence (IPV) for females by age, race/ethnicity, marital status, and household composition. Overall, the report found that the rate of intimate partner violence declined by more than 60% for both males and females. The

majority of the decline occurred from 1994 to 2000, with the rate slowing and stabilizing from 2001 through 2010. The report indicates that from 1994 to 2010, about 4 in 5 victims of intimate partner violence were females; during that period, the rate of female IPV declined from 16.1 victimizations per 1,000 females 12 or older to 5.9 per 1,000. In comparison, male victims of IPV experienced 3.0 victimizations per 1,000 males, declining to 1.1 in 2010.

238.   The second report, <u>Female Victims of Sexual Violence, 1994-2010</u>, focuses on the characteristics of completed and attempted rape or sexual assault against females from 1995-2010. The report examines the nature of violence by weapon use, injury, victim-offender relationship, reporting to the police, and the use of victim services. Overall, the estimated rate of female rape or sexual violence declined by 58%, from 5.0 to 2.1 victimizations per 1,000 females 12 or older. The report also showed that the majority of the victimizations (78%) involved an offender who was a family member, intimate partner, friend, or acquaintance to the victim, with 22% committed by strangers.

Response to issues raised in Question 41(c).
239.   As discussed in response to 41(a), the U.S. government has a long-standing commitment to addressing violence against women. The federal government's efforts to address violence against women in the United States have been guided by two key principles: 1) ensuring safety for victims; and 2) holding offenders accountable.

240.   VAWA has led to significant improvements in the criminal and civil justice systems at the local level – where the majority of these crimes are prosecuted. By forging state, local, and tribal partnerships among police, prosecutors, judges, victim advocates, health care providers, faith leaders, and others, OVW grant programs help provide victims with the protection and services they need to pursue safe and healthy lives, while simultaneously enabling communities to hold offenders accountable for their violence. VAWA funds have supported significant improvements in the criminal and civil justice systems, supporting specialized responses for law enforcement and prosecution. Specialized law enforcement units with dedicated staff that deal exclusively with sexual assault, domestic violence, dating violence, or stalking often produce better outcomes for victims, police, and prosecution. VAWA funds also support critically important training for judges as well as the development of dedicated domestic violence courts that tend to process cases more efficiently and increase offender compliance.

241.   DOJ's Office for Victims of Crime (DOJ/OVC) provides funding to each state to support victim compensation programs pursuant to the Victims of Crime Act (VOCA), 42 U.S.C. 10602. These programs offer compensation to victims and survivors of victims of criminal violence including domestic violence. Compensation programs reimburse victims of crime for medical expenses, mental health counseling, lost wages and funeral expenses. Each state must submit an annual performance report on their VOCA-supported compensation program(s). The quantitative portion of the report includes payment statistics by crime category detailing the number of claims paid and the total amount paid during the reporting period for assault, homicide, sexual assault, child abuse, drunk driving, other vehicular crimes, stalking, robbery, terrorism, kidnapping, arson, and other crimes. Domestic-violence-related claims are shown as a subcategory within the various crime types. In 2011, the most recent data available for a complete year, states paid more than 36,000 domestic violence claims. Complete statistics on compensation provided to victims, including victims of domestic violence can be found on the DOJ/OVC Web page at www.ojp.usdoj.gov/ovc/.

42. The Committee expressed its concern about reports of brutality and use of excessive force by law enforcement officials and ill-treatment of vulnerable groups, in particular racial minorities, migrants and persons of different sexual orientation (para. 37). Such concerns have also been voiced by the Committee on the Elimination of Racial Discrimination and the Human Rights Committee (CERD/C/USA/CO/6, para. 25, and CCPR/USA/CO/3/Rev.1, para. 30). Please:

(a) Describe steps taken to address this concern. Do these steps include establishing adequate systems for monitoring police abuses and developing adequate training for law enforcement officials? Furthermore, please indicate steps taken by the State party to ensure that reports of police brutality and excessive use of force are independently, promptly and thoroughly investigated and that perpetrators are prosecuted and appropriately punished. Information should also be provided on the impact and effectiveness of these measures in reducing cases of police brutality and excessive use of force.

(b) Provide information on measures taken by the State party to put an end to racial profiling used by federal and state law enforcement officials. Have the federal Government and state governments adopted comprehensive legislation prohibiting racial profiling? Statistical data should also be provided on the extent to which such practices persist, as well as on complaints, prosecutions and sentences in such matters.

Response to issues raised in Question 42(a).

242.   The U.S. Constitution and federal statutes prohibit racially discriminatory actions by law enforcement agencies, see, e.g., the Pattern or Practice of Police Misconduct provision of the Violent Crime Control and Law Enforcement Act of 1994, 42 U.S.C. 14141, and the Omnibus Crime Control and Safe Streets Act of 1968, 42 U.S.C. 3789d, which authorize the Attorney General to bring civil actions to eliminate patterns or practices of law enforcement misconduct, including racial discrimination. DOJ also has authority under 18 U.S.C. 242 to initiate criminal investigations of the conduct of individuals acting under color of law who violate the constitutional rights of individuals, including the use of excessive force by any law enforcement officer against any individual in the United States. This law prohibiting excessive force protects members of racial, ethnic, and national minorities to the same extent that they protect every other individual. DOJ has successfully prosecuted law enforcement officers and public officials where sufficient evidence indicates that they willfully violated a person's constitutional rights.

243.   This issue is addressed further, with particular attention to racial and ethnic minorities and undocumented migrants crossing U.S. borders, in the 2013 CERD Report, ¶¶ 90-93 incorporated herein by reference. That discussion, which applies equally regardless of a person's sexual orientation or gender identity, provides a list of available remedies, depending on the circumstances, and addresses training and investigations and enforcement by both DOJ and DHS.

244.   In order to address police brutality and discriminatory conduct, the United States has stepped up its training of law enforcement officers with a view to combating prejudice that may lead to violence. Those efforts, in both DOJ and DHS, are discussed in the 2011 ICCPR Report ¶ 661, incorporated herein by reference.

245.   In addition, ICE/OPR Management Inspections Detention Oversight monitors ICE's 287(g) program with state and local partners to ensure that participating state and local agencies and personnel comply with the terms of Memoranda of Agreement (MOAs) governing their participation. Pursuant to these MOAs, all law enforcement officers authorized to perform 287(g) program functions must undertake and pass a four-week training course at the ICE Academy, which includes coursework on, among other topics, the ICE Use of Force Policy, multi-cultural communication, and avoiding racial profiling, as well as annual refresher training.

246.   For FY 2009 through 2012, DOJ/CRT, working with the U.S. Attorneys' Offices, charged 254 law enforcement officials for criminal civil rights violations, such as excessive force and sexual assaults, in 177 cases. Additional examples of prosecutions demonstrating the scope of available criminal punishments are provided in the 2011 ICCPR Report ¶ 181, incorporated herein by reference. Cases arising in the aftermath of Hurricane Katrina in New Orleans are discussed in response to Question 51.

Response to issues raised in Question 42(b).

247.   The United States is continuing and intensifying its efforts to end racial profiling – the invidious use of race or ethnicity as the basis for targeting suspects or conducting stops, searches, seizures and other law enforcement investigative procedures – by federal as well as state law enforcement officials. The Equal Protection Clause of the Fourteenth Amendment to the U.S. Constitution prohibits any state from denying any person the equal protection of laws. The Due Process Clause of the Fifth Amendment, which has been interpreted to contain an equal protection guarantee, extends this principle to the federal government. Under equal protection principles, government action is subject to review under a standard of "strict scrutiny" when it makes classifications based on race, national origin, lineage or religion. See, e.g., Chavez v. Illinois State Police, 251 F.3d 612, 635 (7th Cir. 2001).

248.   Efforts to end racial profiling through investigations, enforcement and training by both DOJ and DHS are discussed in the 2013 CERD Report, ¶¶ 80-86 and in the 2011 ICCPR Report ¶ 594-603, incorporated herein by reference. Individual states have also enacted legislation to prohibit racial profiling and have imposed data collection requirements on police officers, as explained in the 2011 ICCPR Report ¶ 604, incorporated herein by reference. At the federal level, a proposed bill entitled the Justice Integrity Act was introduced in the House of Representatives in 2008 but was not enacted.

249.   As to the Committee's request concerning national statistical information, DOJ/BJS produces periodic reports on contacts between the police and the public, allowing some analysis for patterns of profiling. The Justice Integrity Act was introduced in the House of Representatives in 2008 to establish a process to analyze and assess unwarranted disparities but no legislation has been enacted. Further information is provided in the 2011 ICCPR Report, ¶¶ 598 and 482, incorporated herein by reference.

Other Issues

43. Please provide updated information on the State party's position on extending an invitation to the special procedure mandate holders who have requested a visit, especially to the request of the Special Rapporteur on the question of torture to visit Guantánamo Bay, as well as the Special Rapporteur on the promotion and protection of human rights and fundamental freedoms while countering terrorism, the Special Rapporteur on the question of torture, the Working Group on Arbitrary Detention and the Working Group on Enforced or Involuntary Disappearances with regard to their joint study into secret detention. Information should also be provided on the State party's position on extending an open standing invitation to special procedure mechanisms.

250.   Although the United States has not yet issued a standing invitation, it welcomes Special Procedures visits and recognizes that such visits contribute to the robust and successful performance of their mandates, both with respect to the United States and elsewhere around the world. The United States strives to accommodate as many official visits as possible, but the large volume of requests for official visits to the United States requires that visits be staggered for scheduling purposes.

251.   The United States has hosted country visits by twelve Special Procedures since 2007, including most recently, the Working Group on Human Rights and Transnational Corporations (April 22-May 1, 2013). In addition, the United States has hosted informal meetings with Special Rapporteurs in the United States and will continue to engage in an open and transparent dialogue during informal consultations with the Special Procedure mandate holders. The United States has offered several UN Special Rapporteurs, including the Special Rapporteur for Torture, a degree of access to its detention facilities at Guantanamo under conditions consistent with the nature of those facilities (e.g., facility visits do not include private meetings with detained enemy forces), although no one has accepted the offer. Due to its special role under the law of war, the ICRC has full access to the detainees at Guantanamo, including private meetings, and maintains an ongoing dialogue with the United States regarding conditions of confinement and the detainees' overall well-being.

252.   Although the United States would certainly consider a request or requests by the other referenced Special Rapporteurs, it notes that the Joint Study on secret detention was published in January 2010, and the information contributed by the United States to the Joint Study is listed therein. The United States provided further supplemental information on May 9, 2012.

44. Please provide:

      (a) Information on steps taken to become a party to the Optional Protocol to the Convention.

      (b) Clarification of whether the State party is considering becoming a party to the Rome Statute of the International Criminal Court.

Response to issues raised in Question 44(a).

253.   The United States continues to address and deal with any violations of the Convention primarily pursuant to operation of its own domestic legal system. As the United States explained in its previous treaty reports (including the CCD) and in response to questions in this submission, the U.S. legal system affords numerous opportunities for individuals to complain of abuse and to seek remedies for alleged violations. Additionally, numerous mechanisms are available to DOJ to ensure that the civil rights of persons in detention in the United States are protected, and various remedies and protections are available that individuals may seek in federal, state and administrative proceedings. These tools are utilized effectively throughout the U.S. justice system. For these reasons, the United States has not taken steps to become a party to the Optional Protocol.

Response to issues raised in Question 44(b).

254.   The United States is not at this time considering becoming a party to the Rome Statute of the International Criminal Court, but it is engaging with the States Parties to the Rome Statute on issues of concern and supporting its work on a case-by-case basis, as consistent with U.S. laws and policy.

45. Please indicate what steps have been taken by the State party to accept the competence of the Committee under article 22 of the Convention.

255.   As indicated in ¶ 163 of the 2005 CAT Report, at the time of ratification, the U.S. Executive and Legislative Branches gave substantial thought to the question of whether to avail the United States of the procedure set forth in Article 22 and decided against doing so. After further consideration, the United States continues to believe that its legal system affords adequate opportunities for individuals to complain of abuse and to seek remedies. Therefore, the United States will continue to direct its resources to addressing such issues through its domestic procedures rather than making a declaration recognizing the competence of the Committee to

consider communications made by or on behalf of individuals claiming to be victims of a violation of the Convention by the United States.

46. Please indicate any changes in the State party's position on withdrawing its reservations, declarations and understandings lodged at the time of ratification of the Convention.

256. The United States does not have any changes to report with respect to the reservations, declarations, and understandings it lodged at the time of ratification of the Convention.

47. Please provide information on steps taken to establish an independent national human rights institution in accordance with the Paris Principles.

257. Although the United States does not have a single independent national human rights institution in accordance with the Paris Principles, multiple complementary protections and mechanisms serve to reinforce the ability of the United States to guarantee respect for human rights, including through its independent judiciary at both federal and state levels. This issue is discussed in the CCD ¶ 129 and the 2013 CERD Report ¶ 31, incorporated herein by reference.

48. Please clarify the State party's position with regard to the interpretation of "territory under the State party's jurisdiction". Does the State party apply the provisions of the Convention which have been named as applicable to "territory under the State party's jurisdiction" to all persons under the effective control of its authorities, of whichever type, wherever located in the world?

258. Paragraph 6 of this report notes that the report does not address the geographic scope of the Convention as a legal matter, although it comprehensively responds to related questions from the Committee in factual terms. The report does, however, address domestic constitutional and statutory law. It is unlawful for U.S. actors to commit an act of torture, under any circumstances, anywhere in the world. U.S. law also criminalizes acts of torture committed by anyone who is later found present in the United States. Moreover, a number of U.S. laws prohibit cruel, inhuman or degrading treatment or punishment or other mistreatment of individuals under the physical or effective control of U.S. personnel without geographic limitation. For example, the Detainee Treatment Act of 2005 provides that "no individual in the custody or under the physical control of the U.S. Government, regardless of nationality or physical location, shall be subject to cruel, inhuman, or degrading treatment or punishment." DTA § 1003, 42 U.S.C. 2000d. E.O. 13491 also explicitly directs that individuals detained in any armed conflict shall in all

circumstances be treated humanely "whenever such individuals are in the custody or under the effective control" of U.S. personnel or agents or are "detained within a facility owned, operated, or controlled by a department or agency of the United States." In such circumstances, U.S. law and policy thus extend certain protections to persons under the effective control of U.S. authorities outside of territory under U.S. jurisdiction.

49. Please provide updated statistical data, disaggregated by sex, ethnicity and conduct, on:

      (a) Complaints related to torture and ill-treatment allegedly committed by law enforcement officials, and investigations, prosecutions, penalties and disciplinary action relating to such complaints;
      (b) The enforcement of the Civil Rights of Institutionalized Persons Act by the Department of Justice, in particular with respect to the prevention, investigation and prosecution of acts of torture, or cruel, inhuman or degrading treatment or punishment in detention facilities.

Response to issues raised in Question 49(a).
259.   Since 2005 DOJ has convicted, or obtained pleas from, more than 165 officers and public officials for criminal misconduct related to police brutality and excessive force. Many of these defendants were convicted for abusing minority victims. According to statistics compiled by DOJ/BJS, in 2006 there were 7.2 complaints of police use of force per 100 full-time sworn officers among large state and local law enforcement agencies (those employing 100 or more officers). Overall, complaint rates were higher among large local police departments, with 9.6 complaints per 100 full-time sworn officers, than sheriffs' offices (4.2 complaints per 100 full-time sworn officers), or state law enforcement agencies (3.1 complaints per 100 full-time sworn officers). The United States does not keep statistical data of the type requested by the Committee, but has provided further information and examples in response to Questions 32, 42 and 51.

260.   DHS/ICE/OPR investigates allegations of physical assault and excessive use of force by ICE and CBP employees and contractors. ICE/OPR does not collect or store demographic information on the victims of the alleged misconduct but can provide the following information. In FY 2010-2012, ICE/OPR received a total of 304 allegations of physical assault or excessive use of force. 72% of the allegations investigated by OPR involved ICE employees and contractors allegedly abusing or assaulting detainees at detention centers. The remaining 28% involved CBP employees. OPR completed investigation on 286 of the allegations and 18

investigations remain open. Of the 286 investigations completed, 13 allegations were substantiated. Of the 13 substantiated allegations, five resulted in removal or suspension, five resulted in no action, and three remain open. For further information, see response to Question 42(a).

261.   DHS/CRCL also investigates complaints from the public alleging violations of civil rights or civil liberties by DHS personnel, programs, or activities. Such complaints may include allegations of discrimination or profiling on the basis of race, ethnicity, disability, sexual orientation, or religion; inappropriate conditions of confinement while in DHS custody; complaints related to the Department's 287(g) and Secure Communities programs; and other civil rights or civil liberties violations related to a DHS program or activity. As an example, CRCL has investigated a number of complaints alleging disparate treatment of individuals based on sexual orientation while in DHS custody and is working collaboratively with ICE to improve conditions for lesbian, gay, bisexual, and transgender detainees.

262.   Of the 256 complaints CRCL opened in 2012, 59 complaints alleged inappropriate conditions of detention, 13 complaints alleged abuse of authority by DHS employees or contractors, 40 alleged excessive force, and 64 alleged inadequate medical/mental health care. Of these, three were kept by the DHS/OIG for investigation, 69 have since been closed, 147 are pending investigation by CRCL, and 37 were referred to DHS component agencies for factual investigation. Through its complaint investigations, CRCL provides senior leadership of the relevant DHS Components with its investigative conclusions and any applicable recommendations for improving policy, practice, or training. CRCL also notifies the complainant of the results whenever possible.

Response to issues raised in Question 49(b).
263.   DOJ/CRT investigates conditions in state prisons and local jail facilities pursuant to the Civil Rights of Institutionalized Persons Act (CRIPA), and investigates conditions in state and local juvenile detention facilities pursuant to either CRIPA or the prohibition on law enforcement agencies engaging in a pattern or practice of violating peoples' civil rights, 42 U.S. 14141. Examples of cases between 2005 and 2010 are provided in the 2011 ICCPR Report ¶ 224, incorporated herein by reference. Between 2009 and 2012, DOJ/CRT opened seven new investigations under CRIPA, issued 12 findings letters detailing the results of investigations at

adult correctional institutions, and settled at least 10 investigations. As a result, CRT currently has matters related to adult and juvenile correctional institutions in more than 25 states, the Virgin Islands, Guam, and the Commonwealth of the Northern Mariana Islands.

264. Additional information is provided in response to Question 42(a). Investigations related to juvenile facilities are discussed in response to Question 34.

50. Please describe steps taken to establish a federal database to facilitate the collection of statistics and information, as requested by the Committee (para. 42) and the Rapporteur on follow-up in his letter of 8 August 2008.

265. As a result of the decentralized federal structure of the United States, the creation of one unified database would be exceedingly difficult and would not materially contribute to better implementation of the Convention. Instead, federal and state authorities compile relevant statistics, including those mentioned by the Committee, and use them for a wide variety of purposes, including assessing the effectiveness of enforcement.

266. Nevertheless, the United States has developed some databases for particular purposes. For example, the FBI maintains Uniform Crime Reporting (UCR) data, which includes data from federal, tribal, state, and local law enforcement. UCR collects statistics on crimes known and confirmed by law enforcement but does not include adjudication data.

267. In addition, DHS/CRCL has implemented a database tracking system to facilitate tracking of complaints received by CRCL regarding DHS activities. The database aids in tracking and searching for information, and its reporting capabilities enhance case tracking and trend analysis. A separate database used to record and process allegations of misconduct lodged against law enforcement officials assigned to ICE and CBP is maintained by ICE/OPR in the OPR Joint Integrity Case Management System. The Office of Investigations at DHS/OIG maintains a 24-hour complaint hotline that also receives complaints about DHS personnel, procedures, policies and other matters involving alleged violations of civil rights. DHS employees, detainees, and members of the public may lodge complaints on the hotline via e-mail, telephone, facsimile, or postal service mail. The OIG Hotline is widely advertised in facilities that house ICE detainees, to ensure awareness of this crucial safeguard among that vulnerable population. The Hotline is also advertised on various DHS websites, including sites

maintained by ICE, CBP, U.S. Citizenship and Immigration Services, and the Transportation Security Administration. If the Hotline receives a credible complaint of assault, sexual abuse, or other criminal behavior involving violations of civil rights, the matters are investigated by the OIG Office of Investigations. Other allegations involving administrative or systemic civil rights abuses are forwarded to the OIG Office of Inspections, the OIG Office of Audits, DHS/CRCL, or other DHS or U.S. government offices for appropriate review and disposition. In September 2009, the DHS/OIG implemented the Enterprise Data System database, which serves as the repository for all allegations concerning DHS employees and programs, including civil rights allegations that are received through multiple avenues, including the Hotline.

51. Please provide updated information on investigations into alleged ill-treatment perpetrated by law enforcement personnel in the aftermath of Hurricane Katrina.

268.   DOJ/CRT has prosecuted a number of cases involving the New Orleans Police Department (NOPD), including several that involved law enforcement shootings in the wake of Hurricane Katrina and the devastation it caused in the city. Convictions of NOPD officers in connection with shootings on the Danziger Bridge resulting in two deaths, and a separate event resulting in the death of Henry Glover are addressed in the 2011 ICCPR Report ¶ 181, incorporated herein by reference. In recent developments in the latter case, the Fifth Circuit Court of Appeals reversed the conviction of the officer convicted of shooting Glover, ruling that the trial judge had incorrectly allowed the accused shooter to be tried jointly with an officer accused of burning Glover's body. The shooter is scheduled to be tried again in August 2013. The Court of Appeals also remanded the other officer's case for resentencing, which is scheduled for September 2013. In 2011 an NOPD officer was convicted on perjury and obstruction charges for having lied during a civil suit in order to cover up the true circumstances of a police-involved shooting that resulted in the death of Danny Brumfield.

269.   In addition to specific incidents, at the request of the Mayor of New Orleans, DOJ launched a civil pattern or practice investigation of NOPD. In March 2011, DOJ issued an extensive report, including DOJ/CRT's first-ever finding that a police department engaged in gender-biased policing – systemic failure to investigate sexual assaults and domestic violence, as discussed in the 2011 ICCPR Report at ¶ 183, incorporated herein by reference. In July 2012 DOJ/CRT reached one of the most comprehensive reform agreements in its history. The

agreement is a road map to ensure respect for the Constitution, increased public confidence in NOPD, and more effective crime prevention in New Orleans. The agreement was approved by a federal court in January 2013, and the United States and the City of New Orleans are now working on implementing that agreement's requirements.

270.   In the aftermath of Hurricane Katrina, DHS/ICE/OPR received six complaints and DOJ/OIG received three complaints alleging ill-treatment by law enforcement personnel. All complaints were investigated in accordance with standard procedures. None gave rise to prosecution or other sanction of any DHS law enforcement employee.

52. Please provide updated information on measures taken by the State party to respond to any threats of terrorism and please describe if, and how, these measures have affected human rights safeguards in law and practice and how it has ensure that those measures taken to combat terrorism comply with all its obligations under international law. Please describe the relevant training given to law enforcement officers, the number and types of convictions under such legislation, the legal remedies available to persons subjected to anti-terrorist measures, whether there are complaints of non-observance of international standards and the outcome of these complaints.

271.   As discussed in response to Question 9, the United States takes measures to protect itself from threats of terrorism while at the same time preserving safeguards under applicable U.S. and international law. In his May 23, 2013 speech, President Obama reaffirmed the United States' commitment to strike the appropriate balance between security and civil liberties. Torture and cruel, inhumane or degrading treatment or punishment are prohibited in all circumstances by all U.S. government officials.

272.   In the first half of 2011, the White House issued a National Strategy for Counterterrorism and a strategy for addressing violent extremism within the United States, Empowering Local Partners to Prevent Violent Extremism in the United States, followed by a Strategic Implementation Plan, issued in December 2011. The Counterterrorism Strategy is available at www.whitehouse.gov/sites/default/files/counterterrorism_strategy.pdf; the Strategic Implementation Plan for addressing violent extremism is available at www.whitehouse.gov/sites/default/files/sip-final.pdf.

273.   The strategies stressed the essential need "to protect the American people from violence, whether from within or from abroad, while at the same time remaining consistent with our core

values as a nation and as a people." In addressing core values, including respect for human rights and upholding the rule of law, the Counterterrorism strategy explained:

> Our respect for universal rights must include living them through our own actions. Cruel and inhumane interrogation methods are not only inconsistent with U.S. values, they undermine the rule of law and are ineffective means of gaining the intelligence required to counter the threats we face. We will maximize our ability to collect intelligence from individuals in detention by relying on our most effective tool – the skill, expertise, and professionalism of our personnel.

274.   A few days prior to the release of the Counterterrorism Strategy in June, the Assistant to the President for Homeland Security and Counterterrorism John Brennan discussed the Administration's efforts to counter terrorism, stating:

> . . . In the past two years alone, we have successfully interrogated several terrorism suspects who were taken into law enforcement custody and prosecuted, including Faisal Shahzad, Najibullah Zazi, David Headley, and many others. In fact, faced with the firm but fair hand of the American justice system, some of the most hardened terrorists have agreed to cooperate with the FBI, providing valuable information about al-Qa'ida's network, safe houses, recruitment methods, and even their plots and plans. That is the outcome that all Americans should not only want, but demand from their government. . . .

> [R]eformed military commissions also have their place in our counterterrorism arsenal. Because of bipartisan efforts to ensure that military commissions provide all of the core protections that are necessary to ensure a fair trial, we have restored the credibility of that system and brought it into line with our principles and our values. Where our counterterrorism professionals believe trying a suspected terrorist in our reformed military commissions would best protect the full range of U.S. security interests and the safety of the American people, we will not hesitate to utilize them to try such individuals. In other words, rather than a rigid reliance on just one or the other, we will use both our federal courts and reformed military commissions as options for incapacitating terrorists.

275.   Extensive U.S. programs, including training, undertaken to ensure humane treatment by law enforcement officers in all contexts are discussed in response to Question 42. The United States continually reviews its laws and practices to ensure that it is protecting innocent people from violence while at the same time living up to U.S. obligations under the Convention and the historical commitment for fair treatment of all people.

276.   International terrorism investigations conducted by the U.S. government since September 11, 2001, have resulted in hundreds of convictions against defendants for terrorism-related offenses. These convictions were obtained in cases that involved charged violations of federal statutes directly related to international terrorism, as well as cases involving charged violations of other statutes where the investigation involved an identified link to international terrorism. The defendants in these cases have the right to appeal their convictions, and they may also petition for habeas corpus relief.

General information on the national human rights situation, including new measures and developments relating to the implementation of the Convention

53. Please provide detailed information on the relevant new developments on the legal and institutional framework within which human rights are promoted and protected at the national level that have occurred since the previous periodic report, including any relevant jurisprudential decisions.

54. Please provide detailed relevant information on the new political, administrative and other measures taken to promote and protect human rights at the national level, since the previous periodic report, including on any national human rights plans or programmes, and the resources allocated thereto, their means, objectives and results.

55. Please provide any other information on new measures and developments undertaken to implement the Convention and the Committee's recommendations since the consideration of the previous periodic report in 2006, including the necessary statistical data, as well as on any events that have occurred in the State party and are relevant under the Convention.

277.   Throughout this report, the United States has endeavored to respond in full to the questions posed by the Committee under the optional reporting procedures, including new measures and developments. In response to Questions 53-55, the United States observes in addition that the 2011 ICCPR Report contains robust reporting on a host of new initiatives to further promote and protect human rights undertaken by the executive, legislative and judicial

branches of the federal government as well as by state and local governments. The United States has incorporated key paragraphs of the ICCPR report by reference in this report and encourages the Committee to review the 2011 ICCPR Report in its entirety. The United States also refers the Committee to its 2013 CERD Report, containing extensive reporting on continuing U.S. efforts to eliminate racial discrimination; specific aspects of the CERD report are also incorporated by reference into this report.

278. With respect to U.S. efforts to combat torture and cruel, inhuman and degrading treatment or punishment, and related issues raised by the Committee's questions, many such developments have also been specifically highlighted throughout this report. The United States takes this opportunity to underscore:

- On January 22, 2009, his second full day in office, President Obama issued Executive Orders 13491 and 13492. See responses to Questions 4-6, 8, 10, 11, 16, 18-21, 38 & 48.

  o E.O. 13491 directs that individuals detained in any armed conflict shall in all circumstances be treated humanely; instructs that such individuals shall not be subjected to any interrogation technique or approach, or any treatment related to interrogation, that is not authorized by and listed in the Army Field Manual, which explicitly prohibits threats, coercion, physical abuse, and "waterboarding," among other conduct, without prejudice to authorized non-coercive techniques of federal law enforcement agencies; orders the CIA to close as expeditiously as possible any detention facilities it operated; requires that all agencies of the U.S. government provide the ICRC with notification of, and timely access to, individuals detained in armed conflict; and ordered the establishment of the Special Task Force to ensure that U.S. transfer practices comply with the domestic laws, U.S. international obligations, and humane transfer policies of the United States. The President accepted the recommendations of the Special Task Force, including those aimed at clarifying and strengthening U.S. procedures for obtaining and evaluating diplomatic assurances from receiving countries for those transfers in which such assurances are obtained, strengthening internal agency oversight of transfer practices, and providing for monitoring in situations where diplomatic assurances are warranted.

- o E.O. 13492 directed the closure of the detention facility at Guantanamo and instituted a review of all detainees held in that facility. That process, although challenging, remains underway.

- The U.S. Supreme Court has determined that constitutional habeas corpus review extends to noncitizens detained by DoD at Guantanamo (Boumediene v. Bush, 553 U.S. 723 (2008)) and to U.S. citizens held in effective U.S. custody in Iraq (Munaf v. Geren, 553 U.S. 674 (2008)). See responses to Questions 8 and 12.

- In July 2009, DoD made more robust its review procedures for individuals held at the Detention Facility in Parwan (DFIP) at Bagram Airfield, Afghanistan. DoD subsequently transferred all Afghan prisoners at the DFIP to Afghan custody on March 25, 2013. See response to Question 5(c).

- In August 2009, the U.S. government established the High-Value Detainee Interrogation Group (HIG) to improve the U.S. ability to interrogate the most dangerous terrorists by bringing together the most effective and experienced interrogators and support personnel to conduct interrogations in a manner that will continue to strengthen national security consistent with the rule of law. See response to Question 21.

- Also in August 2009, the Attorney General ordered a preliminary review into whether federal laws were violated in connection with interrogation of specific detainees at overseas locations. On June 30, 2011, DOJ announced that it was opening a full criminal investigation into the deaths of two individuals in CIA custody overseas, and that it had concluded that further investigation into the other cases examined was not warranted. The two criminal investigations were closed in 2012 after DOJ determined that admissible evidence would not be sufficient to obtain and sustain a conviction beyond a reasonable doubt. See response to Question 23(b).

- In October 2009 Congress enacted the Military Commissions Act of 2009 (MCA 2009), which made many significant changes to the system of military commissions, including prohibiting the admission at trial of statements obtained by use of torture or cruel, inhuman, or degrading treatment, except against a person accused of torture or such treatment as evidence that the statement was made. See responses to Questions 8(b) & 29.

- Through E.O. 13567, issued March 7, 2011, President Obama established a new periodic status review process for detainees at Guantanamo who have not been charged, convicted, or designated for transfer. See response to Question 8(c).

- In March 2011 the United States confirmed its support for Additional Protocol II and Article 75 of Additional Protocol I to the 1949 Geneva Conventions, which contain fundamental humane treatment protections for individuals detained in international and non-international armed conflicts. See response to Question 5(b).

- In the spring and summer of 2011, the White House issued a National Strategy for Counterterrorism and a strategy for addressing violent extremism within the United States, Empowering Local Partners to Prevent violent Extremism in the United States, followed by a Strategic Implementation Plan, issued in December 2011. These strategies confirm the U.S. commitment to countering terrorism in a manner that promotes and protects human rights consistent with U.S. obligations under domestic and international law. See response to Question 52.

- On May 23, 2013, President Obama reiterated his commitment to close the Guantanamo detention facility and outlined a series of steps that have been or will be taken to reach this goal, including calling on Congress to lift the restrictions on detainee transfers from Guantanamo; asking DoD to designate a site in the United States where military commissions can be held; appointing new, senior envoys at DOS and DoD who will be responsible for negotiating the transfer of detainees; and lifting the moratorium on detainee transfers to Yemen. See responses to Questions 8, 8(b) and 52.

ANNEX A

QUESTION 32 (B) SEXUAL VICTIMIZATION OF INMATES

I. <u>Adult Inmates</u>

<u>DOJ/BJS Reporting under PREA</u>

As indicated in response to Question 32(b), DOJ/BJS prepares reports under PREA providing statistical review and analysis of the incidence and effects of prison rape. On May 16, 2013, BJS released its most recent report on sexual victimization in prisons and jails, based on its third National Inmate Survey (NIS-3), conducted from February 2011 through May 2012, <u>Sexual Victimization in Prisons and Jails Reported by Inmates, 2011–12 (2013 BJS NIS Report)</u>, available at <u>www.bjs.gov/content/pub/pdf/svpjri1112.pdf</u>. The report is based on a survey of 92,449 adult inmates held in 233 state and federal prisons, 358 local jails, and 15 special confinement facilities (operated by U.S. Armed Forces, Indian tribes, or ICE). The prevalence of victimization, as reported by inmates during a personal interview, is based on sexual activity in the 12 months prior to the interview or since admission to the facility if less than 12 months. The report explains that "since participation in the survey is anonymous and reports are confidential, the survey does not permit any follow-up investigation or substantiation of reported incidents through review. Some allegations in the NIS-3 may be untrue. At the same time, some inmates may not report sexual victimization experienced in the facility, despite efforts of survey staff to assure inmates that their responses would be kept confidential."

Based on the data sample from NIS-3, BJS estimated that 80,600 inmates in all U.S. jails and prisons experienced sexual victimization by another inmate or facility staff during the 2011-12 period. These figures translate to 4.0 % of the state and federal prison population and 3.2 % of the jail population, which is statistically consistent with past surveys. Among state and federal prison inmates, 2.0% reported an incident involving another inmate, 2.4% reported an incident involving facility staff, and 0.4% reported both an incident another inmate and staff.

The 2013 report provides information on prevalence from the data collected in NIS3, as well as for the two preceding surveys, as summarized in the chart below, 2013 BJS NIS Report at 10 (table 2).

Prevalence of sexual victimization across inmate surveys, by type of incident
National Inmate Surveys, 2007, 2008-09, and 2011-12

Type of incident (see definitions below)	Percent of prison inmates				Percent of jail inmates		
	NIS-1 2007	NIS-2 2008-09	NIS-3 2011-12		NIS-1 2007	NIS-2 2008-09	NIS-3 2011-12
Total	4.5%	4.4%	4.0%		3.2%	3.1%	3.2%
Inmate-on-inmate	2.1	2.1	2.0		1.6	1.5	1.6
Nonconsensual sexual acts	1.3	1.0	1.1		0.7	0.8	0.7
Abusive sexual contacts only	0.8	1.0	1.0		0.9	0.7	0.9
Staff sexual misconduct	2.9	2.8	2.4		2.0	2.0	1.8
Reported as unwilling activity	1.7	1.7	1.5		1.3	1.5	1.4
Excluding touching	1.3	1.3	1.1		1.1	1.1	1.0
Touching only	0.4	0.4	0.4		0.3	0.4	0.3
Reported as willing activity	1.7	1.8	1.4		1.1	1.1	0.9
Excluding touching	1.5	1.5	1.2		0.9	0.9	0.7
Touching only	0.2	0.3	0.2		0.2	0.2	0.1

Note: Detail may not sum to total because inmates may report more than one type of victimization. They may also report victimization by both other inmates and staff.
Terms and Definitions

Sexual victimization —all types of sexual activity, e.g., oral, anal, or vaginal penetration; hand jobs; touching of the inmate's buttocks, thighs, penis, breasts, or vagina in a sexual way; abusive sexual contacts; and both willing and unwilling sexual activity with staff.
Nonconsensual sexual acts —unwanted contacts with another inmate or any contacts with staff that involved oral, anal, vaginal penetration, hand jobs, and other sexual acts.
Abusive sexual contacts only—unwanted contacts with another inmate or any contacts with staff that involved touching of the inmate's buttocks, thigh, penis, breasts, or vagina in a sexual way.
Unwilling activity—incidents of unwanted sexual contacts with another inmate or staff.
Willing activity—incidents of willing sexual contacts with staff. These contacts are characterized by the reporting inmates as willing; however, all sexual contacts between inmates and staff are legally nonconsensual.
Staff sexual misconduct
—includes all incidents of willing and unwilling sexual contact with facility staff and all incidents of sexual activity that involved oral, anal, vaginal penetration, hand jobs, blow jobs, and other sexual acts with facility staff.

II. Juvenile Inmates

In 2013 BJS issued a report based on its second National Survey of Youth in Custody (NSYC), carried out in 2012. This report covered a sample of 8,707 juveniles in state-owned or -operated juvenile facilities and locally or privately operated facilities that held adjudicated youth under state contract. Based on this sample, BJS estimated that 1,720 of the total population held in such facilities (9.5 %) experienced sexual victimization. Sexual Victimization in Juvenile Facilities Reported by Youth, 2012 (2013 BJS NSYC Report) at 6, 9. This was a decline from 12.6% of youth reporting such victimization in the first NSYC, carried out in 2008-2009. See 2013 BJS NSYC Report at 10 (table 2).

The report provided the following information on prevalence of sexual victimization reported by youth by type of incident. 2013 BJS NSYC Report at 9 (table 1). The full report is available at www.bjs.gov/content/pub/pdf/svjfry12.pdf.

Youth reporting sexual victimization, by type of incident
National Survey of Youth in Custody 2012

Sexual victimization	National Estimate	
	Number	Percent
U.S. total	1,720	9.5%
Youth-on-youth	450	2.5
Non-consensual sexual acts	300	1.7
Other sexual contacts only	110	0.6%
Staff sexual misconduct	1,390	7.7
Force reported	630	3.5
Excluding touching	550	3.1
Other sexual contacts only	40	0.2
No report of force	850	4.7
Excluding touching	770	4.3
Other sexual contacts only	70	0.4

Note: Detail may not sum to total because youth may have reported multiple victimizations or due to item non-response. Youth were asked to report on any victimization involving another youth or facility staff in the past 12 months or since admission to the facility, if less than 12 months.

Definition of terms
Youth-on-youth—excludes acts in which there was no report of force.
    Nonconsensual sexual acts—includes contact between the penis and the vagina or the penis and the anus; contact between the mouth and the penis, vagina, or anus; penetration of the

anal or vaginal opening of another person by a hand, finger, or other object; and rubbing of another person's penis or vagina by a hand.

Other sexual contacts only—includes kissing on the lips or other part of the body; looking at private body parts; showing something sexual, such as pictures or a movie; and engaging in some other sexual act that did not involve touching.

Staff sexual misconduct

Force reported—includes physical force, threat of force, other force or pressure, and other forms of coercion, such as being given money, favors, protections, or special treatment.

ANNEX B

ACRONYMS USED IN THIS REPORT

ACA	American Correctional Association
ADA	Americans with Disabilities Act
ANDF-P	Afghan National Detention Facility-Parwan
AUMF	Authorization for Use of Military Force 2001
CCD	Common Core Document of the United States
CAT	Convention Against Torture and Other Cruel, Inhuman or Degrading Treatment or Punishment
CEJA	Civilian Extraterritorial Jurisdiction Act (not enacted)
CERD	International Convention on the Elimination of All Forms of Racial Discrimination
CIA	Central Intelligence Agency
CRIPA	Civil Rights of Institutionalized Persons Act of 1980
DFIP	Detention Facility in Parwan at Bagram airfield, Afghanistan
DHS	U.S. Department of Homeland Security
DHS/CRCL	Office for Civil Rights and Civil Liberties in U.S. Department of Homeland Security
DHS/ICE	U.S. Immigration and Customs Enforcement in U.S. Department of Homeland Security. For offices within ICE, see ICE.
DHS/OIG	Office of Inspector General in U.S. Department of Homeland Security
DHS/OPR	Office of Professional Responsibility, U.S. Immigration and Customs Enforcement in U.S. Department of Homeland Security
DoD	U.S. Department of Defense
DOJ	U.S. Department of Justice
DOJ/BJS	Bureau of Justice Statistics in U.S. Department of Justice
DOJ/BOP	Bureau of Prisons in U.S. Department of Justice
DOJ/CRT	Civil Rights Division in U.S. Department of Justice
DOJ/HRSP	Human Rights and Special Prosecutions Section, U.S. Department of Justice, Criminal Division
DOJ/OIG	Office of Inspector General in U.S. Department of Justice
DOJ/OVC	Office of Victims of Crime in U.S. Department of Justice
DOJ/OVW	Office of Violence Against Women in U.S. Department of Justice
DOS	U.S. Department of State
DTA	Detainee Treatment Act of 2005
ED	U.S. Department of Education
EMD	Electro Muscular Disruption Device
FARRA	Foreign Affairs Reform and Restructuring Act 1998
FBI	Federal Bureau of Investigation in U.S. Department of Justice
HHS	U.S. Department of Health and Human Services
HIG	High Value Detainee Interrogation Group
ICCPR	International Covenant on Civil and Political Rights
ICE	U.S. Immigration and Customs Enforcement in U.S. Department of Homeland Security

ICE/CBP	U.S. Customs and Border Protection in U.S. Department of Homeland Security, U.S. Immigration and Customs Enforcement
ICE/IHSC	Health Services Corps in U.S. Department of Homeland Security, U.S. Immigration and Customs Enforcement,
ICE/OPR	Office of Professional Responsibility in U.S. Department of Homeland Security, U.S. Immigration and Customs Enforcement
ICE/USCIS	U.S. Customs and Immigration Services in U.S. Department of Homeland Security, U.S. Immigration and Customs Enforcement
ICRC	International Committee of the Red Cross
ISAF	International Security Assistance Force in Afghanistan
JJDPA	Juvenile Justice and Delinquency Prevention Act
MCA 2006	Military Commissions Act, 2006
MCA 2009	Military Commissions Act, 2009
NCCHC	National Commission on Correctional Health Care
NCVS	National Crime Victimization Survey, Bureau of Justice Statistics in U.S. Department of Justice
NDAA	National Defense Authorization Act
NIS	National Inmate Survey, Bureau of Justice Statistics in the U.S. Department of Justice
NOPD	New Orleans Police Department
NPREC	National Prison Rape Elimination Commission
NSYC	National Survey of Youth in Custody, Bureau of Justice Statistics in th the U.S. Department of Justice
PBIS	Positive Behavioral Interventions and Supports Center in U.S. Department of Education
PBNDS	Performance Based National Detention Standards, U.S. Department of Homeland Security, Immigration and Customs Enforcement
PBNDS 2011	Revised Performance Based National Detention Standards (2011), U.S. Department of Homeland Security, Immigration and Customs Enforcement
PRB	Periodic Review Board for Guantanamo detainees
PREA	Prison Rape Elimination Act of 2003
SMTJ	U.S. Special Maritime and Territorial Jurisdiction
VAWA	Violence Against Women Act of 1994
VAWA 2013	Violence Against Women Reauthorization Act of 2013
VOCA	Victims of Crime Act 1984